Mediate Your Life
Training Manual

5th edition

Mediate Your Life Training Manual
Fifth Edition

Mediate Your Life
P.O.Box 3539
Amherst, MA 01004

http://www.mediateyourlife.com
connect@mediateyourlife.com

ISBN-10: 098997202X
ISBN-13: 978-0-9899720-2-4

ACKNOWLEDGMENTS

Many people had a hand in bringing this manual into existence and in revising it for this fifth edition.

First, we thank the participants from our workshops and immersion programs. For over a decade, you have let us know what best contributes to your learning and also what doesn't. Your feedback has strengthened this manual and the ways we use it in our trainings.

It was Rowena Finnane who first proposed that we create a manual and who skillfully pulled together the first edition. Julie Stiles transcribed, drafted, and edited contributions to both the first and second editions. In 2011, the "curriculum team"—Laurie Breitner, Mary Sitze, Ania Mills, Lori Woodley, Ann Salsbury, and curriculum design consultant, Ana Sanjuan—spent long hours gathering, updating, and revising the material to better meet the needs of adult learners. Laura MacKay, Fred Levine, and Trisha Thompson copyedited the second edition. Kristen Winstead gave the manual its distinctive design, and continues to offer her invaluable assistance with content and design updates.

The revisions to the fourth edition took place as we were completing *Choosing Peace,* the first volume of our multi-volume series *Mediate Your Life: A Guide To Removing Barriers to Communication.* The fourth edition might never have seen the light of day without the contributions of Mary Sitze and Julie Stiles. We wish to thank Mary for her insight and organization of that revision effort. To Julie, thank you very much for all that you have contributed to this project and to the writing efforts that we have been involved in since 2004.

The fifth edition has again been a collaborative effort with Jocelyn Ruggiero, Kelly Edreich, and Julie Stiles, with design again by Kristen Winstead.

Lastly, with profound gratitude, we thank Marshall Rosenberg, creator of Nonviolent Communication and the model of mediation that is the foundation on which we have built our training. He mapped the territory. We are grateful to Marshall for all that he has provided for us and so many others around the world through his work.

With our warm appreciation,

John Kinyon and Ike Lasater
December 2014

Contents

4. TEMPORAL CONTEXTS OF MEDIATION

5. OTHER MAPS OF THE INTEGRAL GRID

6. PROFESSIONAL DEVELOPMENT

7. PRACTICING TOWARD YOUR GOALS

8. RESOURCES

9. APPENDIX

Chapter 1

Introduction

ABOUT THE MEDIATE YOUR LIFE IMMERSION PROGRAM

To be truly at ease with yourself and those around you is transformative. The first step is to approach every conflict—whether internal or external—as an opportunity. When we understand and communicate our needs with clarity, and with empathy for the universality of those needs, conflict leads to connection. The illusion of separation from self and others fades. Finally, we are at home in the world.

In this manual, we present a simple yet powerful process for learning these vital steps and applying them to daily life. John Kinyon and Ike Lasater's Mediate Your Life approach builds on the work of Nonviolent Communication (NVC) founder Marshall Rosenberg. John and Ike studied with Marshall individually for many years. In 2003, the two men began collaborating on their own innovative techniques for applying the language of needs and the skills of NVC to mediating all aspects of conflict: internal, interpersonal, and external. For people around the world, Ike and John's approach has been the key to learning a new way to communicate and to navigate conflict—as well as a new way to live.

At its core, the Mediate Your Life program is about listening to—and really hearing—ourselves and others. It is about becoming fluent in the "language of needs" and increasing our capacity for empathy so that, out of conflict, a true dialogue and new possibilities can emerge. This approach is reflected in many traditions, old and new:

> **" Grant that I may not so much seek . . . to be understood, as to understand."**
>
> —*From "The Prayer of Saint Francis"*

> **" Seek first to understand . . . then to be understood."**
>
> —*From Steven Covey's* The Seven Habits of Highly Effective People

John and Ike's Mediate Your Life approach grew out of their concerns about pressing global conflicts and their desire to use mediation and the principals of NVC to help humankind shape a better future. However, building that better future begins with mediating the conflicts within our own heads. We cannot hope to understand others until we understand ourselves.

We all have within us a fight/flight/freeze impulse in the face of conflict. This is a natural and predictable part of what it means to be human. But there are reliable ways to return ourselves to a state of self-connection, which is to say a state of presence or equilibrium. The Mediate Your Life immersion program seeks to integrate thousands of years of spiritual and scientific inquiry into what could be thought of as a manual for the human operating system. The immersion program offers a framework of "maps" for navigating difficult situations. These maps represent learnable skills that can be used in any setting and on any scale. When practiced, they produce dramatic results.

LEARNING BY IMMERSION

❝ I've met many people who tried for years to integrate NVC into their lives and found that the yearlong Mediate Your Life program was the missing link for them. This approach gets the fundamental skills and consciousness of NVC much deeper into your bones."

—*Newt Bailey, NVC trainer and founder of The Communication Dojo*

Mediate Your Life's yearlong immersion program provides a dynamic, flexible learning environment built around (1) self-paced, step-by-step learning; (2) extensive role-plays that mimic real-world situations; and (3) learning communities for structured practice that supports participants' growth between multiday intensives and (ideally) long into the future.

Why immersion? Learning to respond to conflict in a new way is very much like learning a new language. And the best way to become fluent in a language is to immerse oneself in an environment where others are speaking and learning it too. Through its three multiday intensives and the structured practice in between, the immersion program offers in-depth training in a new language, a new set of skills, and a new consciousness. It gives participants the time they need to become confident and effective in dealing with all aspects of conflict, in all aspects of their lives.

Watching an experienced trainer put Mediate Your Life skills into action can make those skills appear seamless or even magical. It may appear that the trainer possesses an innate gift for conflict resolution. But MYL skills are entirely learnable when they are broken down and mapped into discrete steps.

The immersion program equips its participants with these learnable skills and demonstrates how to use them holistically over the full spectrum of potential conflicts. It builds systematically on itself. Participants learn how to mediate their own lives by applying new skills and NVC language to resolving their internal and interpersonal conflicts. In this way, they begin to create the lives that they want and are able to find more flow, presence, and enjoyment.

By working to create shifts in their internal experiences, participants discover that their external experiences start changing as well. Mahatma Gandhi famously reminds us that we must "be the change [we] wish to see in the world." The Mediate Your Life immersion program naturally follows that injunction by encouraging participants to draw on internal mediation skills for the benefit of both themselves and their communities. In all three intensives, participants take on the role of mediator in role-play exercises designed to increase their capacity for helping other people to have the kinds of conversations and connections that they seek. In this way, participants deepen and reinforce their personal mediation practice while also learning the skills of the formal or informal mediator.

With each gathering, the program goes deeper. Committed participants can develop sufficient mastery to teach others how to mediate their lives and how to be Mediate Your Life practitioners. Drawing on their personal mediation practice and experience, they learn to coach individuals and lead groups to develop their Mediate Your Life skills.

It takes effort to maintain fluency in a new language and a new consciousness, especially when these feel counterintuitive in many contexts of our present culture. The structured practice times between intensives are therefore as important as the three in-person intensives. Mediate Your Life is pleased to offer a community of fellow learners who support each other's practice and growth, both during the immersion intensives and after.

The immersion program approach was designed in the spirit of ongoing collaboration. A trainer may be at the front of the room in this program, but everyone contributes to the learning. The immersion program is an ever-changing, ever-richer sum of the contributions of a diverse and growing community.

LEARNING FRAMEWORKS

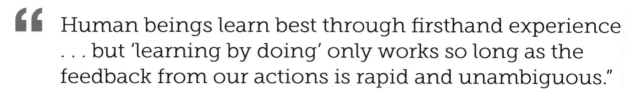

" Human beings learn best through firsthand experience . . . but 'learning by doing' only works so long as the feedback from our actions is rapid and unambiguous."

—*Peter Senge, MIT Sloan School of Management*

The immersion program is built on five learning frameworks:

1. EXPERIENTIAL LEARNING:
THE THREE-CHAIR MODEL

John and Ike developed the three-chair model to create an experiential learning environment that offers real-time feedback, in-the-moment coaching, and self-directed learning. Participants "mediate their lives" by putting the real conflicts from their own lives "into the chairs" (see p. 5.7). They learn by doing and receive feedback from multiple perspectives. For optimal learning, participants rotate positions in conflict role-play situations. Everyone has an opportunity to play mediator and disputant. The participant who is sitting in the mediator's chair will practice staying present and connected with themselves. They will get real-time coaching from the trainers, as well as feedback from those in the disputant roles and from those who are observing the exercise. Both disputants and observers eventually move into the mediator's chair, where they can put into practice all that they have just learned.

2. PRACTICE IN A "FLIGHT SIMULATOR":
DIALING THE LEVEL OF DIFFICULTY TO STAY IN THE LEARNING ZONE

The immersion program is designed to allow participants to select the level of challenge and complexity. In the three-chair model and other experiential activities, participants can dial the level of difficulty. This ability to customize the exercises optimizes learning by ensuring that each participant will be neither bored nor overwhelmed, but

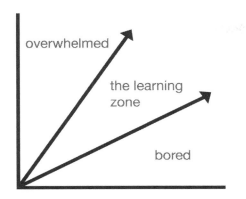

will instead stay right in their learning zone. We think of the role-play practice as akin to learning to fly a plane in a flight simulator. In the simulator, you can pause the role-play at any time to dial the challenge level up or down, get support, or have a "do-over" to immediately integrate information learned through trial and error.

3. CUSTOMIZING THE LEARNING TO MEET INDIVIDUAL NEEDS

Participants inevitably find opportunities to apply what they are learning in the intensives to real-life conflicts. This is ideal, because the opportunity to "mediate one's life" within a safe learning environment helps build capacity to use these skills "in the wild"; i.e., outside of the immersion program with others who are not familiar with NVC or Mediate Your Life. Participants may begin the immersion program by hewing closely to the maps and methodologies that we offer. As their confidence grows, however, they may find their own ways of applying the Mediate Your Life skills and of making meaning from them. We encourage this evolution. In his book *On Becoming a Person*, Carl Rogers, the founder of client-centered therapy, observed that the only learning that significantly influences behavior is "self-discovered, self-appropriated learning." We invite participants to make the MYL approach their own, just as we urge them to tell us how we can best meet their learning needs.

4. USING MEDIATE YOUR LIFE SKILLS TO FACILITATE LEARNING AND GROUP DECISION MAKING

We practice what we teach! The trainers commit to using and modeling the skills offered in this program to facilitate learning and group decision making. In this way, we can deliver on our intentions to create an atmosphere of safety and connection and to foster enjoyment of the learning process. We encourage

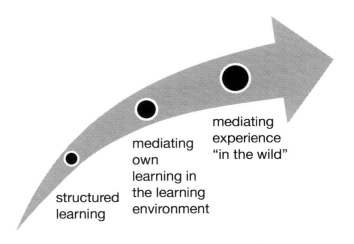

participants to use the skills they are learning to help ensure that they receive what they most want from the intensives and the immersion program experience as a whole.

5. HARVESTING THE LEARNING

At the end of each session, we "harvest the learning" by soliciting feedback on how members of the group experienced the session. This is a time for participants to express what specifically did or did not meet their needs and to make any learning requests. We continually emphasize that ours is a living, breathing program that is meant to evolve with and adapt to the participants in each intensive. We encourage participants to make requests in order to meet their needs and enrich their experiences.

PROGRAM GOALS

Mediate Your Life supports people in mediating conflict between warring parts of themselves, between self and others, and between others.

After the first workshop, participants will be asked to:

- set up and participate in weekly triad practice
- meet weekly with a dyad practice partner
- do a daily self-connection practice

By the end of the yearlong immersion program, our goal is for participants to be:

- significantly more confident and more at ease in dealing with conflict in their lives
- using Mediate Your Life skills in personal and professional situations to more effectively resolve their conflicts, heal their relationships, and contribute to the well-being of those around them
- helping others who are in conflict, either formally or informally
- creating communities of support to manifest and sustain their skills

Participants in our yearlong immersion program report:

- a positive change in how they understand and respond to conflict
- an increased capacity for ease in the midst of conflict
- an increased capacity to empathize with self and others in difficult situations
- an increased ability to return to presence when confronted by what before had seemed overwhelming

Our goals for the next five years include the following:

- Mediate Your Life trainings will be happening in as many languages as possible around the world.
- Participants who become trainers in this work will be leading Mediate Your Life trainings and programs around the world.
- Participants who become mediators will develop their individual practices and gain access to a worldwide peer network.
- As more and more people develop NVC and Mediate Your Life skills, the practice and philosophy behind the skills will become an embedded cultural norm in organizations, communities, and families across the world.

NVC AND A LANGUAGE OF NEEDS

NVC founder Marshall Rosenberg observed that judgments are tragic expressions of unmet needs. At the core of NVC is an awareness that all of us, at any given moment, are trying to meet our needs. If we are not aware of our needs, we tend to spend most of our time just reacting to each other, and this creates all kinds of havoc.

On the other hand, if we're consciously choosing how to think and act, then we can be much more effective—in both resolving difficulties and getting our needs met. We can take the concept of universal needs and turn that into a language that helps focus how we talk to others, how we talk to ourselves, and how we listen to ourselves. Tuning in to the language of needs produces a staggering shift. Suddenly, universal human needs are no longer a source of conflict, but a place of connection that washes away the illusion of our separateness.

See p. 8.1 for a list of useful resources for learning Nonviolent Communication.

OBSERVATIONS, FEELINGS, NEEDS, REQUESTS

In NVC terminology, observations, feelings, needs, and requests (OFNR) are the four components of communication. Having names for these four components helps us to listen and to express ourselves in ways more likely to meet our needs.

EXAMPLE OF USING OFNR

"When I see you rearranging the documents on my desk (observation), I am concerned (feeling) because I would like understanding (need) for what it's like for me when I can't find what I'm working on. Therefore, would you check with me before rearranging my desk (request)?"

Observations vs.	Evaluation and Judgment
• Describing what happened • Seeing things as they are (video camera-like) • Quoting what was said "When you left the room and shut the door so hard the whole room shook . . ."	• Thinking about it, diagnosis • Interpretation, analysis • Deciding who is right or wrong, good or bad, or who is to blame "When you slammed the door . . ."
Feelings vs.	Faux Feelings
• Happy, sad, glad, mad, etc. • Bodily sensation • Emotion ". . . I felt a tightness in my throat and felt sad and frustrated."	• Words we use as feelings that have judgments of the other person implied in them ". . . I felt abandoned."
Needs vs.	Strategies
• Universal, all humans have the same needs • No person, place, or thing attached "I wanted mutual understanding and closure."	• Specific actions, people, or things are means for meeting needs "Will you spend the next 15 minutes brainstorming how to fix this situation?"

Requests	vs.	Demands
• Doable • Present tense • Expressed in action language "Would you be willing to tell me what you just heard me say? And how you feel about it?"		• Use guilt, fear, shame, or denial of choice "And don't you ever, ever slam a door like that again!"

Reflection: OFNR

Think of a situation in which you were mildly triggered. As if you were a video camera, describe in neutral words what stimulated you to be triggered; that is, without judgment. This is your observation. Once you have your observation, look at the list of feelings on the next page and select one or more feelings that arise in you when you think about what happened. Then look at the list of needs and determine what need or needs of yours were not met in this situation. For the last step, think of something you would like to ask of the other that would help meet your unmet needs.

Below is a step-by-step process that you can complete with your own example:

Observation: When I see/hear . . .

Feeling: I feel . . .

Need: because I need . . .

Request: Would you be willing . . . ?

NOTES

FEELINGS AND NEEDS LISTS

Feelings

Frustrated
Impatient
Irritable
Annoyed
Agitated
Disgusted

Sad
Lonely, heavy
Hurt, pain
Brokenhearted
Despairing
Sorrowful

Scared
Terrified
Startled
Nervous
Desperate

Overwhelmed
Shocked
Exhausted
Helpless
Listless
Tired

Confused
Hesitant
Distressed
Embarrassed
Suspicious
Puzzled

Peaceful
Calm
Content
Satisfied
Relaxed
Quiet, still

Affectionate
Warm
Tender
Appreciative
Friendly
Loving, happy

Glad
Excited
Joyful
Delighted
Confident

Playful
Energetic
Expansive
Adventurous
Mischievous
Alive, lively

Interested
Inspired
Intense
Curious
Surprised
Fascinated

Needs

Well-being	Connection	Expression
Sustenance	Love, acceptance	Celebration, play
Nourishment	To matter	To see/be seen
Safety, security	Nurturance	Authenticity
Protection	Intimacy, friendship	Autonomy
Health, wellness	Respect, consideration	Freedom
Movement, recreation	Equality, communion	Choice
Rest	Community, belonging	Meaning
Balance, order	To know/be known	Creativity
Ease, flow	Cooperation, support	Contribution
Peace, harmony	Presence, awareness	Inspiration
Touch	Understanding, clarity	Humor
Growth, learning	Honesty, trust	Passion
Efficacy	Purpose	Integrity
Wholeness	Power, influence	Gratitude
Beauty	Inclusion, mutuality	

A feeling is a reaction to something that is going on within us, such as a thought or a physical injury, or outside of us, such as being stalked by a saber-toothed tiger. Feelings are internal and almost immediate indicators of needs met and needs unmet. Needs refer to those things that are important to human beings universally. They are what we would all like to have in order to survive and thrive in this world.

Feelings are the way the nonverbal systems in our brains tell us their interpretation of what is going on in and around us. When we notice what we are feeling, we are paying attention to a report from an interpretive process that has already taken place. If we are feeling afraid, the nonverbal parts of us are interpreting the available data very differently than if we are feeling happy. Naming and paying attention to our feelings is a way of gaining some access to this nonverbal assessment system. The premise is that these systems (and there are most likely more than one in each of us) are assessing whether we are okay, and whether we are going to be okay. The feelings are the responses to these questions. With our conscious- and language-based mind, we can usefully convert these questions into the question of what needs are or are not being met.

Our feelings are giving us clues we can use to answer that question, with cognition. This gives us important additional information with which to navigate our internal and external worlds. When we have this additional information, we don't have to react to our feeling states with our habitual patterns of action, the early versions of which we learned in childhood. Instead, we can examine our lives with an eye to how we can better meet our needs and the needs of others. In doing so, we can choose to try something different than our patterns would ordain, and learn from the experience. This process of personal learning gives us insight not only into ourselves, but also into the interior lives of others. So, feelings can be seen as a doorway to learning deeply about ourselves and about others.

When needs are met:

Stimulus (observation): When you delivered your report to me two days before the date that we agreed to . . .
Feeling: . . . I was surprised and happy . . .
Need: . . . because with the extra time, I am confident I can deliver the quality I want.

When needs are *not* met:

Stimulus (observation): When you arrive 15 minutes after we agreed to meet . . .
Feeling: . . . I am frustrated and angry . . .
Need (unmet): . . . because I would like respect for how I use my time.
Request: I would have preferred that you let me know as soon as you realized that you were going to be late to our appointment. Would it work for you to do this in the future?

NOTES

Reflection

In this moment, write down how you are feeling. What needs of yours are met? And what needs of yours are unmet? Take a couple of minutes to share this with a partner.

FAUX FEELINGS

Faux feelings reflect not pure feelings. They are stories we have in our heads. They imply that someone else is in the wrong or deserves blame. Faux feelings are tricky, because they are often preceded by the phrase "I feel . . . ." The first column of the table below lists examples of faux feelings. The second column suggests the feelings the speaker may be experiencing when referencing the faux feeling. The third column suggests the needs behind the speaker's faux feeling.

NOTES

Faux Feelings	Feelings	Needs
Abandoned	Terrified, hurt, bewildered, sad, frightened, lonely	Nurturing, connection, belonging, support, caring
Abused	Angry, frustrated, frightened	Caring, nurturing, support, well-being
(Not) accepted	Upset, scared, lonely	Inclusion, connection, community, belonging
Attacked	Scared, angry	Safety
Belittled	Angry, frustrated, tense, distressed	Respect, autonomy, to be seen, acknowledgment
Betrayed	Angry, hurt, disappointed, enraged	Trust, dependability, honesty, honor

Faux Feelings	Feelings	Needs
Blamed	Angry, scared, confused, antagonistic, hostile	Accountability, causality, fairness, justice
Bullied	Angry, scared, pressured	Autonomy, choice, safety, consideration
Cheated	Resentful, hurt, angry	Honesty, fairness, justice, trust, reliability
Coerced	Angry, frustrated, frightened, thwarted, scared	Choice, autonomy, freedom, act freely
Cornered	Angry, scared, anxious, thwarted	Autonomy, freedom
Criticized	In pain, scared, anxious, humiliated	Understanding, acknowledgment, recognition
Discounted	Hurt, angry, embarrassed, frustrated	Need to matter, acknowledgment, inclusions
Disliked	Sad, lonely, hurt	Connection, appreciation, understanding
Distrusted	Sad, frustrated	Trust, honesty
Dumped on	Angry, overwhelmed	Respect, consideration
Harassed	Angry, frustrated, pressured, frightened	Respect, space, consideration, peace
Hassled	Irritated, distressed, angry, frustrated	Serenity, autonomy, calm, space
Ignored	Lonely, scared, hurt, sad, embarrassed	Connection, belonging, inclusion, community
Insulted	Angry, embarrassed	Respect, consideration, acknowledgment
Interrupted	Angry, frustrated, resentful, hurt	Respect, to be heard, consideration
Intimidated	Scared, anxious	Safety, equality, empowerment

Faux Feelings	Feelings	Needs
Invalidated	Angry, hurt, resentful	Appreciation, respect, acknowledgment, recognition
Invisible	Sad, angry, lonely, scared	To be seen and heard, inclusion, belonging
Isolated	Lonely, afraid, scared	Community, inclusion, belonging, contribution
Left out	Sad, lonely, anxious	Inclusion, belonging, community, connection
Let down	Sad, disappointed, frightened	Consistency, trust, dependability
Manipulated	Angry, scared, powerless, thwarted, frustrated	Autonomy, empowerment, trust, equality, freedom
Mistrusted	Sad, angry	Trust
Misunderstood	Upset, angry, frustrated	To be heard, understanding, clarity
Neglected	Lonely, scared	Connection, inclusion, participation, community
Overpowered	Angry, impotent, helpless, confused	Equality, justice, autonomy, freedom
Overworked	Angry, tired, frustrated	Respect, consideration, rest, caring
Patronized	Angry, frustrated, resentful	Recognition, equality, respect, mutuality
Pressured	Anxious, resentful, overwhelmed	Relaxation, clarity, space, consideration
Provoked	Angry, frustrated, hostile, antagonistic, resentful	Respect, consideration
Put down	Angry, sad, embarrassed	Respect, acknowledgment, understanding
Rejected	Hurt, scared, angry, defiant	Belonging, inclusion, closeness, to be seen

Faux Feelings	Feelings	Needs
Ripped off/screwed	Angry, resentful, disappointed	Consideration, justice, fairness
Smothered/ suffocated	Frustrated, scared, desperate	Space, freedom, autonomy, authenticity
Taken for granted	Sad, angry, hurt, disappointed	Appreciation, acknowledgment, recognition
Threatened	Scared, frightened, alarmed, agitated, defiant	Safety, autonomy
Trampled	Angry, frustrated, overwhelmed	Empowerment, connection, community, to be seen
Tricked	Embarrassed, angry, resentful	Integrity, trust, honesty
Unappreciated	Sad, angry, hurt, frustrated	Appreciation, respect, acknowledgment
Unheard	Sad, hostile, frustrated	Understanding, consideration, empathy
Unloved	Sad, bewildered, frustrated	Love, appreciation, empathy, connection
Unseen	Sad, anxious, frustrated	Acknowledgment, appreciation, to be heard
Unsupported	Sad, hurt, resentful	Support, understanding
Unwanted	Sad, anxious, frustrated	Belonging, inclusion, caring
Used	Sad, angry, resentful	Autonomy, equality, consideration, mutuality
Victimized	Frightened, helpless	Empowerment, mutuality, safety, justice
Violated	Sad, agitated, anxious	Privacy, safety, trust, space, respect
Wronged	Angry, hurt, resentful, irritated	Respect, justice, trust, safety, fairness

This list was developed in the April 2000 Wisconsin International Intensive, edited by Susan Skye.

During the mediation process, faux feelings are a signal to the mediator to try to understand the speaker's true feelings and unmet needs. When we, as mediators, can hear the unmet needs of the speaker, we can try to help the speaker to feel heard by the other person in the mediation. If we treat the faux feeling (which is actually a thought or a story) as a true feeling, then we are supporting a sense of continued division or disconnection. Really hearing and focusing on the unmet needs can serve as a starting point toward growing understanding and connection.

Reflection

NOTES

Review the list of faux feelings on the preceding pages. As you read each one, see if you can recall a situation when you used that faux feeling to describe your experience. Now look at the list of feelings next to the faux feeling and see if any of those might fit for you in that situation. Finally, look at the list of needs on the same row and see if any of these are needs that were not met for you in your situation. Do you notice anything different when you identify the feeling and the unmet need vs. the faux feeling? Write down your experience.

THE FOUR COMMUNICATION CHOICES

When we use a language based in human needs, at each moment we can draw on NVC's four communication choices. Two of these focus attention on ourselves; two focus on the other person. When we focus our attention on what is going on inside us, we can do so silently or out loud. Likewise, when we focus on what is going on in the other person, we can keep our guesses to ourselves or guess out loud. Central to all four choices is bringing our attention to the present moment, to what is happening now inside us and others.

The four communication choices:

- **Self-empathy (silent/focused on self)**
  Silently naming our own observations, feelings, needs, and requests (OFNR).
  This is the foundation for empathy and expression with others.

- **Self-expression (out loud/focused on self)**
  Expressing our observations, feelings, and needs and requesting what we would like without blame, criticism, or demand.
  "Classical" NVC construction: "When I see ____, I feel ___ because I'm needing ___. Would you be willing to _____?"
  "Idiomatic/street" NVC: Expressed in natural language that springs from self-empathy.

- **Empathy (silent/focused on the other)**
  Silently guessing the other person's observations, feelings, needs, and requests. This is a way of listening, of placing our attention on another person in an attempt to understand his or her experience.

- **Empathy (out loud/focused on the other)**
  Asking the other person what they are experiencing in the current moment; that is, listening for and guessing the other person's observation, feelings, needs, and requests, taking care to do so without intending blame, criticism, or demand.

EXAMPLE:

Julie calls her friend Tracey on the phone.

Tracey: "Hello."

Julie: "Hi, Tracey, it's me, Julie. How are you?"

Tracey: "Why are you calling now? You missed my birthday, and I haven't heard from you in months. I figured you didn't care anymore."

Julie begins considering the four communication choices.

Self-empathy (silent/focused on self)
"I am hearing Tracey say that I missed her birthday, I am feeling embarrassed, and I have a need for connection. My request to myself is that I consider each of the four communication choices in hopes that Tracey and I will meet our needs for connection."

Empathy (silent/focused on the other)

"I am hearing Tracey say that she figured I didn't care anymore. I wonder if she is feeling sad or hurt and if she wants to know she matters and is cared about."

Self-expression (out loud/focused on self)

"Tracey, I'm embarrassed about that because our connection really matters to me. Would you be willing to talk about this with me for a few minutes?"

Tracey: "Okay, I am willing to talk for a few minutes, and I am really upset."

Empathy (out loud/focused on the other)

"Thanks, Tracey. I am really grateful that we can talk about this. I am hearing that you are really upset. Are you feeling hurt because you want to know you matter and are cared about by your friends?"

The conversation could continue with Julie using these four choices until each person has a sense that she has been heard and understood by the other in the way she wants to be.

	Silent	Out loud
Me	**Self-empathy** Naming to ourselves our observations, feelings, needs, and requests (OFNR)	**Self-expression** Saying how we are and requesting what we would like without blame, criticism, or demand
Other person	**Empathy** Guessing the OFNR of the other	**Empathy** Guessing how another is feeling and what they might be requesting without blame, criticism, or demand

For a deeper explanation of empathy, the elements of empathy, and empathy guesses, please see the section "The Nine Mediation Skills," on page 38.

Chapter 2

A Mediate Your Life Approach to Mediating Conflict

WHAT CREATES CONFLICT?

Brain research shows that we human beings are "hardwired" to experience empathy with one another and to relate in cooperative ways, particularly with those closer to us. This tendency is reflected in the world's spiritual and wisdom traditions. So how do we humans get into such destructive conflicts?

There seem to be two aspects to the eruption of human conflicts. One is a clash of people's strategies for meeting their needs; that is, differences in their thoughts, beliefs, and actions. The other springs from hurt or injury that some people experience as a result of other people's actions. Often this involves a triggering of past hurt and pain, perhaps going all the way back to childhood. When these two aspects are in play—conflicting strategies and the stimulation of hurt—some people may respond with "power-over" strategies (guilt, shame, punishment, reward) or simply become defensive. When this happens, a sense of connection to our shared humanity disappears.

At a cognitive and linguistic level, this process takes the form of moralistic judgments, demands, and "enemy images" (for more on the enemy image, see the "Enemy Image Process," page 75). At a biological level, it is linked to fear and anger and survival mechanisms—the fight/flight/freeze reaction. So much of this happens in automatic, reactive, and unconscious ways. Thus the importance of presence (i.e., mindful awareness) and a language of needs that connects us to what we want and care about (rather than what we're afraid of) as human beings and also to the consciousness of our shared humanity.

Conflict also springs from what it means to be individual biological organisms. Hard as we may try, we cannot experience what another person experiences. Someone can tell us about his experience. He can mime it, dance it, or seek to have us recreate it, but we cannot get inside his nervous system and experience his perceptions, thoughts, or feelings. Hence, we each have our own interpretation of reality. Out of that difference comes misunderstanding. Out of misunderstanding often comes mistrust. Once trust is lacking, it becomes doubly hard to clear up misunderstandings.

Reflection

Take a moment to think about a conflict in your life. Write down your answers to the following questions, and then share them with a partner. What is the first thing you remember happening? What judgments do you have about it? What feelings arise in you when you say the judgments? What values of yours were not met? What would you have wanted to happen differently?

THE INTEGRAL GRID: A MAP OF MAPS

The approach to mediating conflict offered in this training is based on shifting from conflict to connection, from the biological fight/flight/freeze reaction (and the thinking and language that goes with this) to presence and connection with self and other. From this connection, new possibilities can emerge. In our training, this approach is offered as a framework that includes **two dimensions of mediation.**

The first dimension relates to the personal context in which the mediation is taking place: (1) within oneself (between "warring" aspects or voices within one's own head), (2) between oneself and someone else, or (3) between others (when helping others who are in conflict, either formally or informally). Another way to think about this is in terms of first-person, second-person and third-person conflicts.

NOTES

The second dimension has to do with temporal contexts: before, during, and after the mediation—when preparing for a difficult conversation, having the conversation, and then afterward, learning from what happened in the conversation.

These dimensions and their contexts can be represented by a grid of nine spaces. We call this the Integral Grid. In these grid spaces, we have placed "maps" that guide a person in responding to a conflict in particular context. We believe the maps of the Integral Grid live organically inside all of us, and it is for each of us to discover and clarify for ourselves our understanding of them. The maps of the Integral Grid together form a manual for responding to conflict using the "human operating system." When we are born, we are not issued such a manual. We welcome your feedback on how ours serves you.

THE INTEGRAL GRID

	Before	During	After
Inner	Self-Connection Process (SCP) p. 24	Internal Mediation (IM) p. 96	Chooser-Educator (C-E) p. 98
Inter-personal	Enemy Image Process (EIP) for Yourself p. 75	Interpersonal Mediation Model (IPM) p. 89 Making Amends (MA) p. 91	Mourn/Celebrate/ Learn (MCL) for Yourself p. 84
Between Others (Formal/ Informal)	Enemy Image Process (EIP) for Others p. 75	5-Step Mediation Model (MM) p. 35 Healing & Reconciliation (H&R) p. 90	Mourn/Celebrate/ Learn (MCL) for Others p. 84

AN INHERENT STRUCTURE/DNA

Each map has two phases. We call the first phase **understanding and connection,** which is about understanding the experience and needs of self and other, leading to this mysterious thing we call connection. We call the second phase **emergent solutions.** In this phase, new possibilities and creative solutions emerge out of the connection. We think about this process as a dialectical synthesis of opposing perspectives that "transcends and includes" those perspectives. When we refer to the inherent or implicate structure, we are trying to name something that is common to each of the maps and processes we offer in this training.

Reflection

As you read the rest of this manual and practice the maps, see if you can identify the two phases we are talking about. For example, in chapter 3 we introduce the 5-Step Mediation Model. We consider the first four steps of that map to be the understanding and connection phase; the fifth step is the emergent solutions phase.

SELF-CONNECTION IN THE MIDST OF INTENSITY

The practice of returning to self-connection when experiencing the intensity of conflict is the first and most foundational map of the Integral Grid.

Once the deeper parts of our brain are triggered into the fight/flight/freeze survival reaction, our conscious mind tends to be flooded with thoughts about who is right, who is wrong, and who deserves punishment. In addition, we tend to respond to similar situations according to patterns of thoughts and actions we have developed over the course of our life experience. When we are triggered, it becomes very difficult to apply the language and communication skills we possess.

But when we have a map of self-connection, and especially when we practice it, we can learn to respond more effectively. In the midst of this intensity, we can do specific things to become conscious of the needs we want to meet and how we want to meet them. Drawing from the world's wisdom traditions, from empirical research, and from our own experience, we offer the nonverbal (breath, body) and verbal (needs consciousness) elements of self-connection practice as the foundation of self-connection. We also offer gratitude practice. The ability to access a place of gratitude inside of us when triggered plays an important role in effectively responding to conflict.

We request that you set aside at least five minutes a day for self-connection practice (SCP), and that you practice self-connection as often as you can throughout your day.

Times for self-connection practice:

- Set-aside practice times
- During transitions between activities
- During activities throughout the day
- When you are experiencing intensity

The self-connection process:

1. Breath—Slow and deepen your breathing.
2. Body—Notice the sensations in your body.
3. Needs—Ask yourself what needs would you like to have met now.

INTENSITY PRACTICE DURING SET-ASIDE PRACTICE TIMES

When we're experiencing the intensity of conflict, we become aware of breath, feel the intensity in the body (being present to the sensations and letting go of resistance to the feelings), and connect to needs related to the intensity.

Remember something that triggers you, and then shift to self-connection practice (SCP). Repeat until the reaction lessens or disappears. As a triggering situation is happening, you can frame it to yourself as an intensity practice (IP), by saying something like, "Oh, what's happening right now is an IP."

SCP DURING INTENSITY

As you gain more confidence with your SCP, try it in the midst of real intensity. Notice times when you are feeling intensity and become aware of your breath, feel the intensity in your body (being present to the sensations), and connect to needs related to the intensity.

Between stimulus and response there is a space.
In that space is our power to choose our response.
In our response lies our growth and our freedom."

- Viktor E. Frankl

Gratitude Practice with OFNR

1. Observations: Recall something you or someone else did for which you feel grateful.
2. Feelings: How do you feel now as you think about this?
3. Needs: What needs of yours were met? Imagine them fully met in your life.
4. Requests: Do you have a request?

Dyad Practice: Intensity Exercise, Level 1 A–C

LEVEL 1A—INTENSITY WITHOUT EMOTIONAL CONTENT
1. Using a neutral phrase such as "water is wet," your partner starts with low intensity (volume, tone, body language, etc.) and gradually raises the intensity.
2. Stop your partner when you first notice a reaction in yourself.
3. Do SCP. (Note that your partner may need SCP too!)
4. Repeat as desired.

LEVEL 1B—INTENSITY WITH EMOTIONAL CONTENT
1. Tell your partner your trigger (the "incoming"). See if you want to do SCP before starting.
2. Partner delivers trigger. Start with low intensity and gradually raise it.
3. Stop your partner when you first notice a reaction in yourself.
4. Do SCP.
5. Repeat as desired.

LEVEL 1C—ADDING CONSCIOUSNESS OF CHOOSING RESPONSE TO "OTHER"

1. Partner delivers your trigger. Stop when you first notice a reaction in yourself.
2. Do SCP.
3. Choose what you predict will best meet your needs in this moment:
   a) Empathy (silent or out loud)
   b) Self-expression
4. Repeat as desired.

Dyad Practice: Intensity Exercise, Levels 1–3

LEVEL 1—INTENSITY WITH EMOTIONAL CONTENT

1. Tell your partner your trigger (the "incoming"). Check if you need to do SCP before you start. Sometimes just telling your partner what the trigger is can be triggering. If so, you're already in the exercise and can go straight to step 4.
2. Partner delivers trigger. Start with low intensity and gradually raise it.
3. Stop your partner when you first notice a reaction in yourself.
4. Do SCP outloud so as to include your partner. (Note that your partner may need SCP too!)
5. Repeat as desired.

LEVEL 2—RESPONDING TO THE "OTHER"

1. Partner delivers trigger. Stop when you first notice a reaction in yourself.
2. Do SCP.

NOTES

3. Choose a response that you predict will meet your needs:

    a) Empathy for your partner

    b) Self-expression to your partner

4. Tell your partner your choice.

5. Do the response you chose (use the practice templates if they are helpful to you).

Empathy for the other:

- Are you feeling _____
- because of your needs for _____?

Self-expression:

- When I see _____,
- I feel _____
- because of my needs for _____.
- Would you be willing to _____?

    (connection or solution request)

Two types of connection requests:

Would you say what you're hearing? (reflection)

How do you feel about what I said? (expression)

6. Repeat from the beginning.

LEVEL 3—RESPONDING TO A SECOND TRIGGER

1. Partner delivers trigger.

2. Stop when you first notice a reaction in yourself

3. Do SCP.

4. Decide whether to respond by empathizing with your partner, or expressing to your partner.

5. Tell your partner what you've chosen.

6. Do what you've chosen.

7. Partner responds in a way that's intended as a trigger.

8. Repeat steps 2-7 until you are desensitized to the trigger and you can respond by either empathizing or expressing in ways that you and your partner find connecting.

CHANGING CONFLICT HABITS

In the science of habit change literature, researchers talk about three aspects of habits – the cue, the routine, and the reward. The cue is whatever triggers a habit routine to begin, and the reward is essentially the needs that are satisfied by the mental or behavioral routine. In terms of conflict, we have each developed particular conflict habit patterns of mind, emotion, and behavior from our genes, personal life experiences, and surrounding culture. These habits are also deeply rooted in the biological fight-flight-freeze response. Once triggered, conflict habits run their course automatically and for the most part unconsciously. What research indicates is that the power to change a habit lies in awareness of the cue and replacing the old routine with a new one. We have the power to choose our responses to stressful challenges and create and strengthen the habits we want. In our training, we offer a proven methodology for creating new routines for responding to conflict and stress. These are learnable skills. All it takes is consistent practice!

INSPIRATIONAL QUOTES RELATED TO HABIT CHANGE

 The first part of the brain, the part that shows up first in the womb, the part that was there a million years ago—that's our lizard brain. The lizard brain is in charge of fight or flight, of anger, and of survival. That's all we used to need, and even now, when there's an emergency, the lizard brain is still in charge.

There are several small parts of your brain near the end of your spinal cord responsible for survival and other wild-animal traits. The whole thing is called the basal ganglia, and there are two almond-shaped bits in everyone's brain. Scientists call these the amygdala, and this mini-brain apparently takes over whenever you are angry, aroused, hungry, or in search of revenge.

It's only recently that our brains evolved to allow big thoughts, generosity, speech, consciousness, and yes, art. When you look at a picture of the brain, the new part is what you see: the neo-cortex. That's the wrinkly gray part on the outside. It's big, but it's weak. In the face of screaming resistance from the amygdala, the rest of your brain is helpless. It freezes and surrenders. The lizard takes over and tries to protect itself."

– Seth Godin, Linchpin

AWARENESS OF CHOICE

 Life is a good teacher and a good friend. Things are always in transition, if we could only realize it. Nothing ever sums itself up in the way that we like to dream about. The off-center, in-between state is an ideal situation, a situation in which we don't get caught and we can open our hearts and minds beyond limit. It's a very tender, non-aggressive, open-ended state of affairs. To stay with that shakiness—to stay with a broken heart, with a rumbling stomach, with the feeling of hopelessness and wanting to get revenge—that is the path of true awakening. Sticking with that uncertainty, getting the knack of relaxation in the midst of chaos, learning not to panic—this is the spiritual path. Getting the knack of catching ourselves, of gently and compassionately catching ourselves, is the path of the warrior. We catch ourselves one zillion times as once again, whether we like it or not, we harden into resentment, bitterness, righteous indignation—harden in any way, even into a sense of relief, a sense of inspiration.

Everyday we could think about the aggression in the world, in New York, Los Angeles, Halifax, Taiwan, Beirut, Kuwait, Somalia, Iraq, everywhere. All over the world, everybody always strikes out at the enemy, and the pain escalates forever. Everyday we could reflect on this and ask ourselves, 'Am I going to add to the aggression in the world?' Everyday, at the moment that things get edgy, we can just ask ourselves, 'Am I going to practice peace, or am I going to war?'"

—*Pema Chodron*, When Things Fall Apart

 The secret of happiness is freedom.
The secret of freedom is courage."

— *Alice Herz Sommer, WWII concentration camp survivor*

"I have come to the frightening conclusion that I am
the decisive element.
It is my personal approach that creates the climate.
It is my daily mood that makes the weather.
I possess the tremendous power to make a life
miserable or joyous.
I can be a tool of torture or an instrument of inspiration.
I can humiliate or humor, hurt or heal.
In all situations, it is my response that decides whether
a crisis will be escalated or de-escalated and a person
humanized or de-humanized.
If we treat people as they are, we make them worse.
If we treat people as they ought to be, we can help them become
what they are capable of being."

—*Johann Wolfgang von Goethe*

Chapter 3

Mediating Conflict Conversations Between Others

INTENTIONS AND GOALS

When mediating a conflict conversation between others, we make a very important distinction between the goal of resolution and our intention. The mediator's initial intention is connection—first with himself or herself, and then with the parties. Typically, this kind of connection creates a healing of the harbored hurt that has kept the parties apart. It also creates a collaborative problem-solving that produces much more satisfying resolutions that are much more likely to be enacted in ways agreeable to all the stakeholders. Healing and collaboration are welcomed and nurtured when they arise, but these are not intentions. The intention is connection. The rest flows from this.

With this in mind, we have defined three goals for mediating conflict between others:

1. Help each person become conscious of their own needs.
2. Help each person hear the other's experience and needs.
3. Help each person get clear on what they want to meet their needs.

As we approach mediating a conflict conversation between others, what is our intention? If it is to solve the problem, to find a solution, or to "fix" the situation, it may get in the way of people finding a path to connection with each other, and to new possibilities and solutions.

EXAMPLE IN WHICH THE MEDIATOR HAS AN INTENTION TO FIX:

Mother: "I don't know what to do with my daughter. She never does her homework."

Mediator: "Have you spent time with your daughter to understand what she has to do for her homework?"

Mother: "Uh . . . yes, of course I spend time with her!"

Mediator: [to daughter] "What is getting in the way of doing your homework?"

Daughter:	"I don't want to do it. I want to have fun."
Mediator:	"What if you set a timer and allocated one hour for homework, and then the rest of your evening for fun?"
Daughter:	"There isn't enough time for both."
Mediator:	"Are you sure you are trying hard enough to create time for both?"
Daughter:	"Oh boy, you sound like my mother!"

EXAMPLE IN WHICH THE MEDIATOR HAS AN INTENTION TO CONNECT:

Mother:	"I don't know what to do with my daughter, she never does her homework."
Mediator:	"Are you saying this out of concern for your daughter's future?"
Mother:	"Yes, very much so."
Mediator:	"So, are you saying that when you see your daughter not doing her homework, you become concerned for her?"
Mother:	"Yes."
Mediator:	"And is it that you are motivated to contribute to her well-being?"
Mother:	"Yes, that's it. I worry about how she will do in her life."
Mediator:	[to daughter] "I hear your mother saying she is worried because she cares about you. Would you say what you heard?"
Daughter:	"Yeah, she wants me to do my homework."
Mediator:	"Thank you for saying what you heard. I also heard that she's concerned about your well-being. Are you willing to say you heard that too?"
Daughter:	"Yeah, yeah. She cares about me and worries about me when I don't do my homework."
Mediator:	"Thank you for your willingness to say what you heard. Now, what would you like your mom to hear from you?"
Daughter:	"My schedule is so busy with school, sports, and activities that I don't have enough time to just hang out."
Mediator:	"So, are you saying you want some free time to relax?"
Daughter:	"Yes! You got it."
Mediator:	"I heard your daughter say that she wants some free time to relax. Would you say that back to her to let her know that you heard her?"
Mother:	"Yes, she wants some free time to relax."

Here the mediator is talking to each person with the hope of increasing the connection. The mediator asks both mother and daughter to reflect what the other said in order to help them hear and understand each other.

Map: 5-Step Mediation Model (MM)

The 5-step mediation model (MM) facilitates each person's being heard to their satisfaction. That in turn fosters connection among the parties, out of which tends to emerge a search for resolutions satisfactory to everyone. NVC provides the learnable skills and consciousness to create this kind of connection.

TWO PHASES

1. Understanding and connection phase— supporting each person to connect to needs and hear the other (steps 1–4)
2. Emergent solutions phase—facilitating solution requests and agreements (step 5)

FIVE STEPS

1. Empathize with person A and surface her need(s).
2. Ask person B to reflect A's need(s).
3. Empathize with B and surface his need(s).
4. Ask A to reflect B's need(s).
5. Solution requests and agreements.

NINE MEDIATION SKILLS

1. **Empathy.** When listening to each disputant, mediator can in any moment choose presence, silent empathy, understanding, or need language (OFNR, or observations, feelings, needs, requests).
2. **Connection requests.** Mediator asks each person to reflect, or say back, to the other what they heard, both in terms of understanding and the other's needs. Mediator asks how the person feels having just heard what they heard or said what they said.
3. **Pulling by the ears.** When person does not reflect

back understanding or needs of speaker when asked, mediator asks again if person is willing to reflect the other's needs.

4. **Emergency first-aid empathy.** Mediator switches to empathy upon perceiving that someone is in too much emotional reaction to empathize with the other.

5. **Tracking.** Mediator tracks the flow of the overall process, particularly needs that have been expressed but not yet reflected or addressed by the other.

6. **Interrupting.** Mediator interrupts speaker with intention to connect and contribute to that person and to the overall process.

7. **Self-empathy.** During the mediation, in addition to in-the-moment self-connection practice (SCP), mediator can use OFNR for self-empathy.

8. **Self-expression.** Mediator may express own needs and requests in order to contribute to disputants meeting their needs during the mediation process.

9. **Solution requests**. Mediator helps each person with clarity and specificity of their requests connected to needs. Mediator also holds and frames request vs. demand and seeks to get everyone's needs met (interdependence).

THE "NEED BEHIND THE NO" (NBN) PROCESS OF THE REQUEST PHASE
1. Empathic connection with needs behind the request
2. Empathic connection with needs behind the no
3. Search for reconciling request to meet needs

THREE TYPES OF AGREEMENTS IN THE REQUEST PHASE
1. Main agreements
2. Supporting agreements
3. Remedial agreements

NOTES

The following table gives examples of mediation skills that could be used to respond to an increasing level of challenge when mediating.

Mediation challenges	Skills used
Reconnecting with ourselves as we react to our interpretation of what is going on.	Self-empathy
Empathetically connecting with another person.	Empathy
Empathetically connecting with two or more people who are in a conflict conversation.	Empathy
Asking for reflection, or some other demonstration by the listening party that they have heard the person who has just spoken.	Connection requests
Asking for reflection and person does something other than reflect.	Connection requests Pulling by the ears Emergency first aid Empathy Self-expression
Person starts talking when I am talking or other person is talking.	Interrupting Self-expression Empathy Tracking
Dealing with intensity • **Content intensity**—particular topics are triggering because of your life experiences • **Amplitude**—emotional intensity, loudness, movements	Self-empathy Self-expression Interrupting Empathy

Mediation challenges	Skills Used
Supporting the creation of agreements that are doable and proposed in present-tense, action language.	Solution requests Self-expression Empathy All the other skills
Creating agreements to support the likelihood that the primary agreement will be kept and also what to do if it is _not_ kept.	Solution requests Self-expression Empathy All the other skills

THE NINE MEDIATION SKILLS

SKILL 1: EMPATHY

Empathy, whether spoken or silent, is active. When giving empathy, we strive to be present with ourselves and another. We connect to and demonstrate our understanding of another's feelings and needs in that moment. In this way, we give them a sense of being fully heard and understood. Receiving empathy often helps them to regain connection with themselves and others. It also typically helps them gain understanding about what they need in this situation, what they would like to meet their needs, and what happened to create the conflict.

THE FOUR ELEMENTS OF EMPATHY
1. Presence: Resting pure attention and awareness on the speaker, letting go of thinking; listening from internal stillness, with the heart
2. Silent empathy: Silent thinking about understanding and need language
3. Understanding and meaning: Saying back to the speaker what we are hearing in a way that makes them feel heard about their reality and experience
4. Need language (OFNR): Connecting observations, thoughts, feelings, and wants to needs; deepening or savoring needs; listening for requests

PRESENCE

This element of empathy is about conscious awareness that transcends thinking. It is listening from the heart, from unconditional regard. In presence, we place our witnessing attention on the other person, gently resting our awareness on what we are receiving from them, letting go of thinking about or trying to understand what they are saying.

SILENT EMPATHY

Silently being with the speaker, thinking about what we hear is going on for them and is important to them, and also silently guessing feelings and needs.

UNDERSTANDING AND MEANING

This element of empathy is about reflecting back to the speaker what we're hearing them say in a way we guess that they would like to be heard, in a way that is true for them, for their reality. It is the attempt to reflect back where they are, in language that resonates with them. This is not about agreeing with what they're saying. It is about demonstrating our understanding and acceptance of their subjective frame of reference: reflecting back what they are observing, feeling, and wanting, and perhaps even some of their thoughts, in the form of observing with them their thoughts about the situation. We maintain focus on their internal, subjective frame of reference.

NEED LANGUAGE (OFNR)

This element is about focusing our listening attention and verbal reflection on the needs alive in this person as they are speaking, and connecting their observations, thoughts, feelings, and specific wants to their needs. We might reflect back the feelings and needs we hear in what they are expressing. Or we might guess their thoughts and feelings and translate. Once we have connected with the person's needs, we may wish to linger a bit on them, pausing to savor them with the person. This can be done in silence or by reflecting back, perhaps focusing on slightly different aspects or on the words that seem to resonate most strongly and deeply with them. This makes space for deeper self-connection to happen. After connecting to the needs, we can listen for any requests the person may have of themselves or others.

KEY PRINCIPLES OF EMPATHY

- **The power of the present.** When someone is talking about the past or the future, it can be powerful to focus our listening attention on what is going on in them in the moment, as they're speaking—and experiencing the consequences of their thoughts.

You might say, "So as you think about that, are you feeling _____ (because you're needing) _____?"

- **Empathy vs. expression.** Giving empathy is about the speaker, not us. We stay focused on what is going on for them, what is "alive" in them, rather than sharing what is going on for us. We try to remain clear on the focus and on whether to offer empathy or to self-express to create connection between the speaker and ourselves.

- **Following vs. leading.** We follow what the person says is going on for them rather than leading the conversation toward what we think is important.

- **Connection before outcome.** Empathy occurs when we understand and connect with what is alive for the speaker. It is not about helping them feel better or trying to change anything for them.

- **Be fully with the person's experience.** We follow what the other person reveals, rather than leading them by imposing thoughts on them.

- **Empathy guesses.** We have found that most people do not enjoy being told how they feel. So we guess what the other person's experience is, rather than tell them what we think they are experiencing. We guess because we want to understand. Then we watch the speaker's reaction to see whether our guess was accurate, and we make our next communication choice based on that observation. Empathy guesses are just that—guesses. It helps to stay present, following what the person is saying about their experience now. Worrying about whether our guesses are correct only gets in the way of being able to follow with another guess or reflection.

- **We don't need the details.** Our own need for understanding does not have to be met in order for the speaker's need for empathy to be met. We can guess at their present experience and needs without fully understanding their story. In fact, if we focus on the details of someone's story of the past, we may miss what they are feeling, needing, and wanting in the moment.

- **Empathy is a choice.** During an interaction, there may be times when we do not want to empathize with someone. We may want to focus on self-empathy or express ourselves to them. Empathy is a strategy to meet your needs and the needs of others, one of many in any moment.

- **Empathy takes practice.** Most of us did not learn at our mother's knee how to be present and understand another's experience. Most of us are not accustomed to using language in a particular way to guess what another person is observing, feeling, needing, and wanting. But empathy is a learnable skill. We can practice it, and we can get better at it.

- **What empathy is NOT.** It is not sympathy, "fix-it" advice, reassurance, explaining, educating, correcting, one-upping, storytelling, interrogating, or shutting down.

INSPIRATIONAL QUOTES RELATED TO EMPATHY

EMPATHY AS PRESENCE

> The Chinese philosopher Chuang-Tzu stated that true empathy requires listening with the whole being: The hearing that is only in the ears is one thing. The hearing of the understanding is another. But the hearing of the spirit is not limited to any one faculty, to the ear, or to the mind. Hence it demands the emptiness of all the faculties. And when the faculties are empty, then the whole being listens. There is then a direct grasp of what is right there before you that can never be heard with the ear or understood with the mind."

—*Marshall B. Rosenberg, from* Nonviolent Communication: A Language of Life

EMPATHIC LISTENING

> 'Seek first to understand' involves a very deep shift in paradigm. We typically seek first to be understood. Most people do not listen with the intent to understand; they listen with the intent to reply. They're either speaking or preparing to speak. They're filtering everything through their own paradigms, reading their autobiography into other people's lives. . . .

When I say empathic listening, I mean listening with intent to understand. I mean seeking first to understand, to really understand. It's an entirely different paradigm. . . . In empathic listening, you listen with your ears, but you also, and more importantly, listen with your eyes and with your heart. You listen for feeling, for meaning. You listen for behavior. You use your right brain as well as your left. You sense, you intuit, you feel.

Empathic listening is so powerful because it gives you accurate data to work with. Instead of projecting your own autobiography and assuming thoughts, feelings, motives and interpretation, you're dealing with the reality inside another person's head and heart. You're listening to understand. You're focused on receiving the deep communication of another human soul."

—*Steven Covey*, The Seven Habits of Highly Effective People

" I do not know if you have ever examined how you listen, it doesn't matter to what, whether to a bird, to the wind in the leaves, to the rushing waters, or how you listen in a dialogue with yourself, to your conversation in various relationships with your intimate friends, your wife or husband. If we try to listen, we find it extraordinarily difficult, because we are always projecting our opinions and ideas, our prejudices, our backgrounds, our inclinations, our impulses; when they dominate we hardly listen to what is being said. In that state there is no value at all. One listens and therefore learns, only in a state of attention, a state of silence in which this whole background is in abeyance, is quiet. Then, it seems to me, it is possible to communicate . . . .

Real communication . . . can only take place when there is silence."

—*Krishnamurti*

" Have you ever been surfing? Imagine you're on your surfboard now, waiting for the big one to come. Get ready to get carried with that energy. Now, here it comes. Are you with that energy right now? That's empathy. No words—just being with that energy.

When I connect with what's alive in another person, I have feelings similar to when I'm surfing.

To do this, you can bring in nothing from the past. So the more psychology you have studied, the harder it will be to empathize. The more you know the person, the harder it will be to empathize. Diagnoses and past experiences can instantly knock you off the board. This doesn't mean denying the past. Past experiences can stimulate what's alive in this moment. But are you present to what was alive then or what the person is feeling and needing in this moment?

If you think ahead to what to say next—like how to fix it or make the person feel better—BOOM! Off the board. You're into the future. Empathy requires staying with the energy that's here right now. Not using any technique. Just being present. When I have really connected to this energy, it's like I wasn't there. I call this 'watching the magic show.' In this presence, a very precious energy works through us that can heal anything, and this relieves me from my 'fix-it' tendencies."

—*Marshall B. Rosenberg, "Surfing Life Energy and Watching the Magic Show"*

EMPATHY EXAMPLES AND EXERCISES

The process of empathy can seem to consist mostly of saying what you have heard. Reflecting back both your understanding and the needs you have heard.

EXAMPLE:

Bob arrives home to find his wife, Sue, upset after a conversation with her sister about what to do about their elderly mother. Like many such conversations between Sue and her sister, this one has ended with both of them angry. Bob empathizes with Sue as she tells him what happened:

Sue: "I try to tell her what I think we should do to help Mom, and she keeps interrupting me. She doesn't listen to me, and I get so angry."

Bob: "So when she interrupts you, you feel angry because you would like her to listen to you?"

Sue: "Yes! It's just like when we were kids. She always had her way because she was older. My ideas never mattered to her, and it's no different now."

Bob: "When she interrupts, it reminds you of when you were both younger, and you would really like to be heard for your ideas. Am I getting it?"

Sue: "I do want to be heard, and I want her to acknowledge that my ideas have merit. In fact, sometimes my ideas are better!"

Bob: "So it's not just about being heard, but you'd also like some acknowledgment of the merit of your ideas and that you have something to contribute?"

Sue: "Absolutely. I'd really like what I have to say to matter."

To understand what empathy is, it can be helpful to see what it is not. Imagine the same conversation between Bob and Sue, but with Bob responding in ways that we would not consider empathy.

EXAMPLE:

Bob: "I can relate. If your sister interrupted me like that, I would get angry too."

Bob: "I am angry just hearing about it."

Bob: "You shouldn't let her do that to you."

Bob: "She has been doing it ever since I have known you. When are you going to stand up for yourself?"

Bob: "Well, don't worry. What you say matters to me."

Bob: "You should have more compassion for her. That husband of hers is a windbag. She probably never gets a word in edgewise."

Reflection

NOTES

Review each example of Bob saying something that is not empathetic. How would you name each example? For instance, is it an example of sympathy? Advice? Reassurance?

Awareness Exercise: Empathy

Notice and name what you and other people do instead of empathizing. As you go about your daily life, write down the words you and others use in situations where you or they could empathize but instead do something else. Later, review your notes and name the actions as sympathy, reassurance, or advice. Do this until you notice that you are naming in your head what you and others are doing instead of empathizing at the very moment that it is happening. This kind of awareness is the first step toward learning and change. What you do with it is the subject of this immersion training.

Dyad Practice Exercise: Empathy—The 6-Minute Exercise

Find a partner. Decide who will be the speaker (A) and who will be empathizer (B).

1. For six minutes, A talks about something that is alive and meaningful for her right now.
2. For the first minute, B practices pure presence.
3. For the second minute, B practices silent

NOTES

empathy, guessing understanding and A's OFNR.

4. For the third and fourth minutes, B practices stating understanding and meaning, periodically reflecting back the content of what A is saying.

5. For the fifth and sixth minutes, B practices reflecting back need language and deepening into the needs with what A is saying.

6. Stop and share feedback and reflections on the experience.

7. Switch roles and repeat.

Triad Practice Exercise: Empathy

Find two partners. Decide who will play the roles of disputants A and B, and who will be the mediator. Choose a scenario for the role-play.

1. Mediator asks A what she would like B to hear.

2. While A speaks, the mediator practices presence and silent empathy, alternating between the two.

3. Once A reaches a natural pause, the mediator reflects back the understanding and meaning of what he or she heard.

4. The mediator continues to listen and periodically reflects back what A said in need language (OFNR) and deepening into the needs.

5. When A feels heard, the mediator repeats steps 1–4 with B.

6. Stop and share feedback and reflections on the experience.

7. Rotate chairs, changing roles so there is a new mediator, and repeat steps 1–6.

8. Rotate chairs again, until all three of you have practiced being mediator.

9. Repeat steps 1–6.

SKILL 2: CONNECTION REQUESTS

This skill is used to help people empathize with one another and to hear and understand each other's experiences and needs. A typical connection request is to ask B to reflect back to A what he heard A say about her needs. While still in the beginning stage of the mediation, or if someone is having trouble reflecting, we might reflect back the needs we heard from A and ask B whether he will say that he heard A express those needs. If B reflects back an understanding with no mention of A's needs, then we can reflect back the needs we heard and ask B whether he is willing to reflect the needs back as well. As mediator, we might also check with A and B to see whether what the other just reflected has left each feeling accurately heard.

Another connection request is to ask both A and B how they feel about what they heard the other say.

EXAMPLE:

Mary is mediating between Jim and Phil, longtime friends in conflict over a lakeside cabin they purchased jointly ten years ago.

Mary: "Jim, what would you like to say about the cabin?"

Jim: "Well, I think we need to sell, but Phil wants to hold on as long as possible. The reality is that the cabin and property are losing value in this market, and it needs a lot of work to keep it up. We just don't use it enough to make it worth it."

Mary: "I'm hearing that you want to sell the cabin because it is losing value and needs a lot of work, is that right?"

Jim: "Yes, I mean, I like being there too, but I don't have the time to put into keeping the cabin in good repair, and Phil is happy to use the cabin but hasn't shown any interest in putting work into it. I could use the money we'd get. The property still has significant value left, but most likely it will keep dropping."

Mary: "So it sounds like you would like some companionship in caring for the cabin, but also some financial stability that selling the cabin would give you?"

Jim: "Yes, I mean, he uses the cabin too, but I'm always the one figuring out how to get repairs and upgrades made, and almost always the one doing them. Some help from him would have been nice, but I'm ready to be done with it."

Mary: "Let me make sure I have heard you. Your needs are for contribution, for help in caring for the cabin, and for financial stability?"

Jim: "Yes."

Mary: [turns to Phil] "Phil, I heard Jim say that he has needs for contribution and help in taking care of the cabin, and also a need for financial security. Are you willing to say back to Jim what you heard him say?"

Phil: "Well, yeah, okay. I heard him say he'd like help and partnership taking care of the cabin, and that he's concerned about his finances."

Mary: "Thank you, Phil, for your willingness to do that."

Mary: [turning back to Jim] "Jim, how was that for you to hear?"

Jim: "Okay."

Mary: "Phil, what would you like to be heard about?"

Phil: "I get that Jim's worried about the value going down and all, but I don't want to let go of the cabin. It holds a lot of good memories. Jim and I have done joint trips there every summer with our families. Our kids practically grew up together there. I really wanted us to pass it down to them so they could take their kids, too, someday."

Mary: "So for you the cabin holds a lot of positive memories, and you wanted to be able to contribute to your kids by passing it on to them?"

Phil: "Yes. It's been a place where we have a good time just being together, being with our families and each other. I mean, Jim is like family to me. Giving up the cabin, it's like giving that up."

Mary: "Are you saying that closeness with your family and friends is important to you, and to have a place where you can celebrate the good things in your life, and the cabin has come to represent all of that?"

Phil: "Sure. It's something we all look forward to every year."

Mary: [turns back to Jim] "Jim, I heard Phil say that the cabin for him is about closeness and

---

Typical Connection Requests

"Jim, I heard Phil say that he has a need for X. Are you willing to say you heard him say he has a need for X?"

"Jim, I heard Phil say that he has a need for X. Are you willing to tell Phil what you heard him say about his need for X?"

"Phil, how do you feel hearing Jim say that?" (After Jim has reflected Phil's needs.)

"Phil, how was that for you to hear?" (After Jim has reflected Phil's needs.)

"Jim, how do you feel, having reflected Phil's needs?" (After Jim reflects Phil's needs.)

"Phil, do you feel Jim heard you?"

celebration with family and friends, and it's also a way to contribute to his kids through leaving something with positive memories for them. I'm wondering if you are willing to tell Phil what you heard him say?"

Jim: "Okay. He has lots of positive memories there with all of us and wants to feel close to family and enjoy his life, and he wants to leave it to the kids so they can continue the tradition of going there."

Mary: "Jim, I'm wondering how you feel, having reflected those needs back to Phil?"

Jim: "Well, I get that we've had a lot of good times there. I can see why he wants to hold onto it."

NOTES

Triad Practice Exercise: Connection Requests

Find two partners. Decide who will start the exercise as disputants A and B and who will start as mediator. Choose a scenario for the role-play.

1. Disputant A starts with one or two sentences that she wants to be heard.
2. The mediator translates into needs until A agrees that what the mediator says is what she intended to say about her needs.
3. The mediator turns to B and says, "I heard A has a need for X. Would you be willing to reflect back to A what you heard?"
4. After B reflects A's need(s), the mediator turns back to A and asks, "How do you feel having heard that?" And then back to B and asks, "How do you feel having reflected that?"
5. A and B each respond.
6. Mediator starts with B and repeats steps 1–5.

7. Stop and share feedback and reflections on the experience.
8. Rotate roles so there is a new mediator. Repeat steps 1–6.
9. Rotate roles again so everyone has a chance to mediate. Repeat steps 1-6.

SKILL 3: PULLING BY THE EARS

"Pulling by the ears" is used to help people in conflict demonstrate their hearing and understanding of the other's experience when they do not seem to understand the mediator's request. For example, B might be asked to reflect back A's needs but instead self-expresses or reflects back A's thoughts and judgments. If B self-expresses, we might say that we want to hear more about that later and ask him to say again what he heard A say. If B does reflect back what he heard A say, but what he heard was only thoughts and judgments, or if A reflects back something different than what we heard A say, we could thank B for saying what he heard. Then we could reflect back the needs we heard from A and ask B if he is willing to say these needs back to A. As mediator, we could assure B that he does not have to agree with A's statements, only repeat what he heard. If necessary, we might ask A to repeat what she said. The skill is in supporting each person to demonstrate an understanding of the other's needs to the other's satisfaction. If, in this scenario, B seems too triggered to reflect, we might instead offer B emergency first-aid empathy (skill 4). Pulling by the ears often involves other skills, such as interrupting (skill 6), empathy (skill 1), or self-expression (skill 8).

> ### EXAMPLE 1:

In this scenario, A has expressed a need for respect and consideration. The mediator has asked B to say that he heard A say those were her needs. Rather than reflect A's need, B says that he needs respect too and begins to explain why.

The mediator might say:
"Excuse me, excuse me . . . I do want to hear what you are saying right now. However, before I do that, would you be willing to say back what you heard A say were her needs? I heard her say she has needs for respect and consideration. Would you be willing to say those needs back to A?"

OR . . .
"Would you be willing to tell A what you heard her say about those needs?"

EXAMPLE 2:

In this instance, B has expressed a need for respect and consideration; the mediator has asked A to reflect that. Rather than reflect B's need, A says, "B said that I am inconsiderate and disrespectful."

The mediator might say:
"Thank you for your willingness to say what you heard. I heard him say he wants respect and consideration. Are you willing to say those needs back to him?"

OR . . .
"Thank you for saying what you heard. I also heard him talk about needs for consideration and respect. Would you be willing to reflect the needs he does want to be met, and to leave out any judgments of you?"

OR . . .
"Would you try it again and this time leave yourself out of the need? Try to identify the need that's not being met, without any reference to who will meet it or how."

Triad Practice Exercise: Pulling by the Ears

Find two partners. Decide who will start as disputants A and B and who will start as the mediator. Choose a scenario for the role-play.

1. Mediator requests that disputants, when asked to reflect each other's needs, either express or reflect back judgments.
2. Mediator asks A what she would like B to hear.
3. Mediator empathizes with A, translating what A said into underlying needs.
4. When A indicates that the mediator has heard her needs, the mediator turns to B and asks B to reflect the needs A stated: "B, would you be willing to reflect that back to A what you heard her say and what her needs are?"
5. B self-expresses instead of reflecting as asked.
6. Mediator: "B, I want to hear how you feel about this, but first I wonder if you would tell A the needs you heard her say? I heard her needs were X and Y."
7. B reflects back A's needs.
8. Mediator asks B what he wants to say and empathizes with him, getting to his needs.

9. Mediator asks A if she is willing to reflect back what she heard B say and his needs. A reflects back judgments.
10. Mediator pulls by the ears: "Thank you for being willing to say what you heard. I heard A say that she has needs for X and Y. Would you be willing to say those needs back to her?"
11. A says back B's needs.
12. Stop and share feedback and reflections on the experience.
13. Rotate roles so there is a new mediator. Repeat steps 1-12.
14. Rotate roles again so everyone has a chance to mediate. Repeat steps 1-12.

SKILL 4: EMERGENCY FIRST-AID EMPATHY

As mediators, we may offer emergency first-aid empathy (aka emergency empathy) when one disputant does not empathize with the other when asked to do so. This skill may also be used when one party begins talking while the mediator or the other party is talking. We might respond to the interruption with empathy and then return our focus to the other party. (Skill 5, tracking, addresses that challenge.)

EXAMPLE 1:

Responding to an interruption: "Excuse me . . . Are you feeling urgent to be heard? Do you want to be sure that what you want to say is going to be considered fully?"

EXAMPLE 2:

Responding to B, who has not reflected back A's needs and has instead shared more of his pain about this

NOTES

situation: "Excuse me . . . Are you saying this because you are feeling distressed about the situation too, and you want that to be heard?"

Triad Practice Exercise: Emergency First-Aid Empathy

Find two partners. Decide who will start the exercise as disputants A and B, and who will start as mediator. Choose a scenario for the role-play.

1. The mediator asks the disputants to respond to a request to reflect the other person's needs with a triggered emotional reaction.
2. Disputant A starts with one or two sentences she wants B to hear.
3. The mediator helps to translate these into needs, and A says these are her needs.
4. The mediator turns to B and says, "I heard A has a need for X. Would you be willing to reflect that back to A?"
5. B reacts with an emotional response—judgment, anger, frustration, or irritation.
6. The mediator responds with emergency first-aid empathy, empathizing with B's reaction and translating it into feelings and needs.
7. Mediator starts over with B and repeats steps 2 - 6.
8. Stop and share feedback and reflections on the experience.
9. Rotate roles so there is a new mediator. Repeat steps 1–8.
10. Rotate roles again so everyone has a chance to mediate. Repeat steps 1- 8.

SKILL 5: TRACKING

This skill consists of being aware of where you are in the process or map, for example where you are in the 5-step mediation model, and then making a choice based on that awareness. While the mediation maps are presented in a linear fashion, real conversations rarely proceed that way. So we pay attention to where the conversation leaves the map, choose how to respond, and remember where we were in the 5-step process so we can return to that point if we want to.

For example, if we have asked B to reflect A's needs and instead he reacts and begins to tell his own story, we might choose to give B emergency empathy. Then we can track the fact that B has not yet reflected A's needs and renew that request. We might make other choices as well.

Tracking may go several layers deep. For example, we may decide to give B emergency empathy when he reacts. If A interrupts, we might have to respond in some way to A. Now we are tracking two layers—the empathy and needs for B's reaction and the request for B to reflect A's needs.

With practice, each of us finds what works for us to help with tracking. We might keep brief written notes or use an aid, such as shifting a pen from one side of the table to the other as a reminder of where we are. In transparency, we might self-express (skill 8) that we forgot and ask the disputants for a reminder. Finally, to return self-connection, we might take a moment to give ourselves self-empathy (skill 7). We could suggest that everyone, the mediator and disputants, take a moment to self-connect.

Like most skills, our ability to track improves with practice. We suggest starting with a role-play exercise that encourages the disputants to react and interrupt. When they do, we as mediator can briefly stop the mediation and say out loud on which step it has been paused, our choices for possible responses, and any needs or requests that we are tracking to return to. We suggest beginning with tracking that is only one layer deep. That is, if we are already responding to an interruption or reaction by one disputant, then the other disputant does not interrupt until we have returned to where the mediation left off. When we're more experienced, we may want to practice with two or three layers, with disputants interrupting while we are responding to an earlier reaction.

EXAMPLE:

The mediator renews the request to reflect:

"I am remembering that before you told me what you just told me, I asked you if you would reflect A's needs. I am wondering if you are willing to do that now?"

A interrupts empathy for B. The mediator responds:

"B, I recall you were saying you wanted respect and consideration, and I'm wondering if there is something else you want to be heard about in this situation?"

Once A has received empathy for her interruption, the mediator returns to empathy for B, then asks A to reflect B's needs. The mediator tracks that A has a need that has not been reflected back by B:

"A, I also heard you saying that you had a need for respect, and I'd like to know if you would like that need reflected back by B?"

Triad Practice Exercise: Tracking

NOTES

Find two partners. Decide who will start the exercise as disputants and who will start as mediator. Choose a scenario for the role-play.

1. The mediator asks disputants to "dial the level of difficulty." To raise the level of challenge, they could, for example, interrupt each other during the mediation. To lower the level of challenge, they could agree to always reflect needs after being asked a second time.

2. The mediator starts the mediation, asking, "Who would like to go first?"

3. When someone interrupts or does not do what the mediator requests, the mediator a) pauses the role-play; b) identifies on which step of the 5-step mediation model it has paused; c) states how he or she is going to respond;

d) declares the requests or needs that he or she is tracking to return to later.

4. The mediator resumes role-play and enacts the choice that was made.

5. Once the mediation has returned to the point where the interruption happened, all parties identify the step of the model they last were on, along with the needs and requests they were tracking.

6. Stop and share feedback and reflections on the experience.

7. Rotate roles so there is a new mediator. Repeat steps 1–6.

8. Rotate roles again so everyone has a chance to mediate. Repeat steps 1–6.

NOTES

SKILL 6: INTERRUPTING

This is the skill of interrupting one or both disputants in a way that leads to further connection with them, rather than stimulating disconnection. This skill comes in handy in three scenarios. In the first, both disputants are talking at the same time. In the second, one of the disputants is saying more than we can track, or for other reasons we can't take it all in. In the third scenario, one disputant is offering judgments that will likely be disconnecting and make it difficult for the other to hear.

EXAMPLE 1:

When the disputants are speaking at the same time.
Mediator: "Excuse me, excuse me . . . When you are talking at the same time I can't understand and contribute to your hearing each other the way I would like. So, are you willing to speak one at a time?"

EXAMPLE 2:

When someone is saying more than we can track.
Mediator: "Excuse me, excuse me . . . I want to make sure that I am hearing what you

are telling me. So, I would like to tell you what I have gotten so far. . . . (At this point, we summarize what we have been hearing the person say and conclude by asking if we have been hearing what they wanted us to hear.)

EXAMPLES 3–4:

How we might interrupt a disputant because of concerns about the impact of what that disputant is saying upon the other.

The mediator is empathizing with A. B is triggered and starts expressing.
Mediator: "Are you saying that because of your distress over wanting to be sure you will be heard about how it was for you?"

If the response is yes, the mediator might go on.
Mediator: "I assure you that I want to make sure you are heard. For now, I would like to finish this piece with A, and then I'll come back to you. Are you okay with doing it that way?"

OR . . .
"Excuse me. Are you willing to wait just until I finish hearing this from A?"

OR . . .
"Excuse me. Is it okay with you if I finish hearing A before hearing you?"

Dyad Practice Exercise: Interrupting

Practicing the skill of interrupting with a partner provides an opportunity to try different ways of maintaining connection with the person who is being interrupted.

Find a partner. Decide who will be the speaker, A, and who will be the interrupter, B.
1. A begins speaking about someone in a judgmental and blaming manner.
2. B interrupts and makes an empathy guess about what A is saying, such as, "Excuse me, A, are you distressed about this situation because you are needing X?"
3. A responds according to her feelings.
4. Begin again, with A speaking judgmentally.

5. B interrupts with self-expression, ending on a request, such as, "Excuse me, A, I'm feeling uncomfortable because I'd like care and consideration for all of us. How do you feel, hearing that?"

6. A responds according to her feelings.

7. Stop and share feedback and reflections on the experience. A and B discuss how each choice felt for them.

8. Switch roles and repeat steps 1–7.

SKILL 7: SELF-EMPATHY

During a mediation, we use self-empathy to help reestablish self-connection when working with internal intensity—when we experience a fight/flight/freeze reaction. After we have done some self-connection practice, self-empathy allows us to reconnect more fully by taking time to name to ourselves what we are observing, feeling, needing, and wanting. With enough practice, and depending on the situation and the level of intensity we're experiencing, we can divert part of our attention to silently doing self-empathy while the mediation is happening. Another choice is to ask for a break from the mediation and take some time by ourselves to do self-empathy or call a support person.

Self-empathy helps us return to what is most true to us in our internal experience. During a difficult mediation, we can use it when, for example, we notice that we're having an "enemy image" (judgments, blame, criticism) of a disputant. Another option is to use the enemy image process (described on page 75), of which self-empathy is a part.

When we lose self-connection while mediating, we can use this process to "come back to life," as NVC founder Marshall Rosenberg has said. After we reconnect with ourselves in this way, we can reengage and will likely be more effective in meeting the needs we want to meet.

EXAMPLE:

Joe is mediating a dispute between two business partners who have asked him to help them dissolve their consulting practice. He has already worked separately with each in pre-mediation sessions. In the early stages of the mediation, A says to B, "What you have just said is a classic example of your idiotic way of thinking and why I want out of this business relationship."

The thought flashes through Joe's mind that A's statement is likely to prompt B to react in ways that will create further distance. He imagines that B will be so offended, he might terminate the mediation. Joe thinks, "A just screwed up all the progress we had made. Now I am going to have to clean up the mess she just made."

Joe has an enemy image of A—a perception that she is the problem. If he continues to think that A is the problem, even if he does not express the thought, his demeanor and voice will likely communicate judgment of her, if not specifically this judgment.

If Joe can become aware that this is going on in him, he can quickly do SCP. Then he can choose among the nine mediation skills. Say he chooses self-empathy. In this situation, Joe might think, "When I hear A say this, I feel distressed because I have a need to contribute by supporting people in being heard. And, I realize, I have a need for awareness of the impact of words on others." Having taken a few moments for this internal dialogue, Joe can then choose what to do next.

Self-empathy is done internally. However, practicing aloud with a dyad partner lets us choose the level of intensity of the trigger and receive support in connecting with feelings and needs.

Dyad Practice Exercise: Self-empathy

This is a version of the intensity exercise.

Find a partner. Decide who will practice self-empathy first (A) and who will do the triggering first (B).
1. A gives B a triggering phrase.
2. B delivers the trigger.
3. As soon as A feels discomfort, she stops the role-play and does self-empathy aloud, naming thoughts, feelings, and needs.
4. B gives support in connecting with needs and feelings if requested.
5. Stop and share feedback and reflections on the experience.
6. Switch roles and repeat steps 1–5.

SKILL 8: SELF-EXPRESSION

This skill addresses the challenge of honestly expressing ourselves as mediators while at the same time fostering connection. If one or both disputants are behaving in ways that are not meeting our needs, we may choose to use self-expression first to communicate our feelings and needs, and then to make a request designed to meet them. The skill comes in expressing ourselves honestly and without judgment or demand.

EXAMPLE:

Joe is mediating a dispute between two business partners who have asked him to help them dissolve their consulting practice. He has already worked separately with each in pre-mediation sessions. In the early stages of the mediation, A says to B, "What you have just said is a classic example of your idiotic way of thinking and why I want out of this business relationship."

The thought flashes through Joe's mind that what A has just said will blow up the mediation. He imagines that B will be so offended that he will terminate the mediation. He thinks, "If A would be just more aware of what she says, I would not have to be dealing with the mess she has probably just made."

Joe has an enemy image of A: he is judging her for her conduct. If he continues to think that A is the problem, even if he does not express the thought, his demeanor and voice will likely communicate judgment of her, if not specifically this judgment.

In the example for skill 7, self-empathy, we left off with Joe having done self-empathy. Continuing from there, Joe might then choose self-expression, perhaps saying, "A, when I hear you say things like 'your idiotic way of thinking' to B, I am concerned about the effect this will have on his capacity to listen and his willingness to stay in the mediation. Because I would like to support each of you to be heard, I'd like to know what B said that prompted you to say that about his way of thinking. Would you be willing to say that?" This is self-expression because you are letting A know, from your personal experience as a mediator, your concerns about the effect her words may have on B and on the mediation process. Since you want to express in a way that connects, you then also share your need and make a request.

EXAMPLE:

If B starts talking when Joe is listening to A's response, Joe might say, "Excuse me, B. I really want to hear what you have to say, and I'd like to also understand what A is saying. Would you be willing to have me spend another few minutes with A and then come back to hearing you?"

Note that Joe has other choices here: emergency first-aid empathy (skill 4) or a combination of emergency first-aid empathy and self-expression.

Dyad Practice Exercise: The Watercooler

Find a partner to work with. In this exercise, you and your partner role-play colleagues who meet up at the watercooler during a break. Person A, the initiator, launches into complaints about another colleague or a situation in the office. B practices using self-expression to respond, first doing self-empathy to ensure that the expression comes from connection to himself.

For example, A might say, "Did you know he did it again? He just totally went behind my back to talk to Mary about the new project. He knows it's my project. How dare he? I'd really like to undermine his project."

1. A speaks in judgmental manner about an office situation or colleague.
2. B holds up his hand to stop role-play and do self-empathy out loud.
3. B goes back into role and responds with self-expression, making sure to include the following:
   a) How he feels having heard what A said
   b) What A said that concerns him
   c) What needs he has that are prompting this response
   d) And finally, a request

For example: "I feel worried when I hear you say 'I'd like to undermine his project' because I'd like us all to work together to get things done. How do you feel, hearing me say that?"

4. A responds to request as she feels moved.
5. B responds again with self-expression.
6. Go out of roles and discuss how it felt for both of you.
7. Switch roles and repeat steps 1–5.

Triad Practice Exercise: Self-expression

To practice the skill of self-expression, this exercise has two disputants frequently interrupt and express anger and disconnection with each other or the mediator. When they do, the mediator briefly stops the role-play to do self-empathy and then responds with self-expression.

Find two partners to work with and decide who will start as disputants and who will start as the mediator. Choose a scenario.

1. Mediator starts mediation as usual.
2. As soon as one disputant begins talking over the other or reacts in anger and disconnection, the mediator:
   a) Holds up a hand to signify that they are stepping out of role
   b) Practices self-empathy silently or out loud.
3. Mediator goes back into role and responds with self-expression, ending with a request for one of the disputants.
4. Continue until another opportunity for self-expression occurs, at which point the mediator repeats steps 3–4.
5. Step out of role and reflect on the exercise.
6. Switch roles so there's a new mediator and repeat steps 1–6.
7. Switch roles again and repeat steps 1–6.

SKILL 9: SOLUTION REQUESTS

This skill addresses the final stage of mediation: supporting people in conflict to make clear, effective requests of one another that help them move toward mutually satisfying solutions. It includes developing supporting agreements that help people stick with their main agreement—and also outline actions to take if that agreement is not kept.

Effective solution requests have the following characteristics:

- Doable
- Phrased in the present tense to say what the person wants to happen now
- Expressed using actionable language: what you want, not what you don't want
- Stated as requests, not demands
- Meet everyone's needs, not those of one party over another

Checklist: Suggestions for a Solution Request

☐ Is it doable?
☐ Is it in action language?
☐ Is it present-tense?
☐ Is it stated as a request, not a demand?
☐ Does it seem intended to meet the needs of all, or just one party?
☐ Are supporting agreements in place to help everyone keep the main agreement?
☐ Are restoring agreements in place in case the main agreement is not kept?

EXAMPLE:

To support two people to reach agreements that are most likely to meet the needs of both, the mediator must recognize when they are expressing what they want in negative language, or in a way that is not doable or not in the present tense, or as a demand. The mediator then can help shift those wants into requests that are positive, present, in action language, and are truly requests.

In the following example, Charles is mediating between a couple, Bill and Sue, who have been in conflict over Bill's hectic work and travel schedule. Through the mediation, they have reconnected with each other and are in the final stage of resolution. Here is a snippet of their conversation as Charles supports each of them in making requests.

Charles: "Sue, let me start with you. What is it you would like from Bill?"

Sue: "Well, I just want him to be more considerate, you know. I'd like him to think about me and what I'm going through when he works late or is gone for two weeks out of the month."

Charles: "I hear that you want consideration, and I'm concerned that what you've said is not yet doable. What is something Bill could do that would meet your need for consideration?"

Sue: "Okay, I guess really what I would like is for him to be home by six every night that he's in town."

Charles: "So you would like to ask Bill to be home by six when he is in town. Bill, is that something you are willing to try?"

Bill: "I would like to be with Sue and the kids more. However, there are just times when I feel like I have to stay later to deal with emergencies. So I'm reluctant to say I will be home every night. I could imagine being home by six three nights a week, though."

Charles: "You would be willing to agree to leave work to arrive at home by six three nights a week, then?"

Bill: "Yes."

Sue: "I can see it happening for maybe a week, then he'll slip back into the usual pattern."

Charles: "It sounds like you'd like some trust that Bill means what he says. I do like to stress that requests are always present-tense, so even though Bill is agreeing to actions in the future, what he's actually saying is that he has the present intention to leave work in time to arrive home by six three nights a week. Sue, is there something else you would like to hear from Bill right now that would help you trust in his agreement?"

Sue: "I guess it would help me to hear that he's just as committed to us as he is to his work."

Bill: "Honey, I am committed to you and the kids. I will do what I can to get home for dinner by six, three nights a week."

Mediator Key Phrases

"A, I do not think that's something clear or doable. What do you want B to hear or say back?"

"That's what he could not do, what could he do?"

"What could he specifically do that would meet your need?"

"What request could you make of yourself or someone else to support you in keeping this agreement?"

"How would you like to respond if he does not keep this agreement?"

Charles: "The other piece of what Sue raises, at least in my mind, is the importance of having agreements in place to support this main agreement. So Bill, I'm wondering whether there's something you can request of Sue or someone else that would support you in keeping your agreement?"

Bill: "Well, Sue could stop nagging me when I am not home at six. It doesn't help me want to arrive at home."

Charles: "So you would like her to stop doing that. And would you like that because you would like to be trusted that you want to have dinners with the family?"

Bill: "Yes."

Charles: "Okay, I am clear on what you would like her to stop doing. Is there something you would like her to do instead of what you would like her to stop doing?"

Bill: "Maybe when I walk in she could just connect with me first instead of immediately bombarding me with what I need to do or how frazzled she feels from dealing with the kids."

Charles: "And what would meet your need for that connection with her when you walk in? What could she do specifically that would help you feel connected?"

Bill: "She could, if possible, briefly stop what she's doing, look me in the eye, give me a kiss, and ask me how my day was."

Charles: "Sue, is that something you would be willing to do?"

Sue: "Yes, I would be willing to do that. I'd enjoy that too. Does that really support you to leave work, though?"

Bill: "It might, but you're right, I think there's something I need to set in place to remind me to leave. Maybe I can plan at the beginning of the week which nights I will be home, and then ask my secretary to remind me an hour before I want to leave so I can finish things up."

Charles: "Okay, so you are proposing two supporting agreements. The first is to plan the nights at home for dinner at the beginning of the week. The second is to ask your secretary to remind you an hour before you want to leave for dinner at home at six."

Triad Practice Exercise: Solution Requests

Find two partners to work with and decide who will start as disputants and who will start as mediator. Set up a role-play in which you are beginning the resolution phase with the needs surfaced and the parties already fairly connected to each other.

Choose a scenario to work with and determine the needs on each side.

For example: Imagine a conflict between a teacher and an administrator over the teacher's use of an innovative online program in the classroom. The teacher's needs are for autonomy and to contribute to the children; the administrator's needs are also to contribute to the children, through making sure test scores are high, and for accountability to school boards.

1. Mediator begins the resolution stage of the mediation with disputant A, asking what request she would like to make of B.
2. Disputant A makes request.
3. Mediator holds up hand to step out of role and out loud checks the request.
   a. Is it doable?
   b. Is it positive?
   c. Is it present-tense?
   d. Does it seem like the person is making a demand?
4. Mediator goes back into role and responds to request, supporting A to modify the request.
5. Repeat steps 2–4 as necessary to get to a request that is present-tense, positive, and in action language. (If mediator notices immediately that the request does not comply with a characteristic and can respond right away, he or she should feel free to skip step 3.)
6. Mediator switches to the other disputant and repeats steps 2–5.
7. Step out of role and reflect on exercise.
8. Switch roles so there's a new mediator and repeat steps 1–7.
9. Switch roles again so everyone has a chance to mediate, and repeat steps 1–7.

THE NEED BEHIND THE NO

"The need behind the no" is a core process for the emergent solutions phase.
1. Empathize with the needs behind the request and clarify the request.
2. Empathize with the needs behind the no.
3. Search for a request that reconciles the needs of the parties.
4. Repeat steps 1–3 until a solution emerges.

Triad Practice Exercise: The Need Behind the No

Find two partners. Decide who will start the exercise as disputants and who will start as mediator. Choose a scenario for the role-play.
1. The mediator asks disputant A to state her needs in the conflict and make a request.
2. The mediator helps clarify the request and connects to need(s).
3. The mediator asks B if he feels willing to do A's request, and whether it will meet his needs to do so.
4. B says no in some form. The mediator empathizes, getting to the needs that are keeping B from saying yes.
5. The mediator then asks B if he has a request that would meet his needs and A's needs. The mediator helps B clarify the request.
6. The mediator asks A how she feels about the request and empathizes if there is a no.
7. Repeat the three parts of the process until a solution emerges.

INFORMAL MEDIATION

Sometimes we face the challenge of applying the mediation skills and process when we have not been asked to support others in a conflict conversation. This is informal mediation, or what Marshall Rosenberg calls "sticking your nose into other people's business without being asked." In this context, we are not one of the disputants. We decide to enter into others' conflict to meet our own needs. We probably will have very little time to establish connection with the parties and for them to accept our support. Thus, we should use as few words as possible and also have clarity regarding our own needs and our own requests. Informal mediation draws on all of the nine mediation skills, but in a different order and emphasis than in formal mediation:

1. Empathy guesses and reflections are quicker and briefer, and there is a more rapid back-and-forth empathizing with disputants.
2. Often, more self-expression (particularly transparency and vulnerability) helps people be more trusting and open to receiving our support.
3. We may ask the disputants to reflect back what they're hearing each other say, but later on in the process, probably after a number of rounds of just empathizing with each person.
4. All parts of solution requests and agreements could be there, but be quicker, briefer, and simpler than in formal mediation.

EXAMPLE:

There are many instances in which we might use informal mediation, including in meetings with colleagues, with friends and family, or even with small children who are tussling over a toy or what they are going to do next. The language we use may change depending on the audience, but the dynamic remains constant.

Imagine you are with a father, Bob, and his son, Jim, and they have exchanged several barbed comments. These are dear friends of yours. Hearing what they have said, you notice how uncomfortable you feel. Another moment of self-reflection reveals that your discomfort is arising out of your need for care and harmony. In the next moment, you conclude that you also have a need to help. (Hey—you just did self-empathy on the fly!) So you say the following, "Jim are you feeling frustrated here because you would like respect for your choices?" Then, without waiting for Jim to respond, you turn to Bob and say, "And Bob, are you irritated because you would like respect for your life experience?" If they seem to be responding positively, you could continue offering brief empathy guesses and reflections to both.

If they don't seem to be responding positively, you could try self-expression, saying something like, "I care so much about both of you, and I feel sad hearing the tension between you. I'd love to support you both in feeling heard and connecting with each other. How would it be for you if I continued to see if I'm understanding what you're both saying?"

If that goes well, then at some point you could say something like, "I've also found that letting each other know what you're hearing from the other can be helpful. Would you like to give it a try?" If they say yes, then you could help them do this. You also might be able to help with the solution phase by asking if either one of them has something they want to offer or ask of the other that might work for both of them, and then help them with solution requests and getting to agreements.

A note of caution: It is important that we be mindful of our own physical safety when entering into others' conflicts, particularly if we do not know the disputants and how they might react. It's best to practice informal mediation in safe environments, such as with business colleagues and among family.

A tip on body language: The "stop" or "talk-to-the-hand" sign of the upheld palm may have the unintended consequence of escalating the conflict, because some people react out of their need for autonomy. However, most people do not object to a straight extended hand: a relaxed hand with the thumb up, held straight out from the wrist.

Triad Practice Exercise: Hand Gestures for Informal Mediation

1. Two disputants will dial the difficulty of a sample dispute, deciding ahead of time if they will be talking over each other.

2. The informal mediator practices using the hand gesture along with saying, "Excuse me," as many times as necessary to get the attention of the disputants. Practice using the gesture without conveying any sense of demand or urgency.

PRACTICE AND FEEDBACK

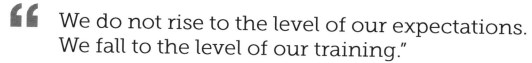

We do not rise to the level of our expectations. We fall to the level of our training."

—*Archilochus, Greek soldier and poet, c. 650 BC*

We see the intensives as a place to learn what and how to practice, be inspired, and find community. However, the long-lasting learning, growth, and change that we've seen happen is through regular practice and as a result of effective, supportive feedback from dyad and triad partners.

DEBRIEFING AND "BIOFEEDBACK"

Giving and receiving feedback is an essential component of learning and change. In the training, we see it as a kind of "biofeedback": we describe our internal experience in relation to another's actions. We see three key aspects to this:

1. Debriefing: How was it for you? What happened for you during the exercise or role-play?
2. Feedback on needs met:
   a) Start with what you liked, what worked for you, what was connecting. Try to find at least one thing to say, however small.
   b) Give specific observations.
   c) Share your internal experience, feelings, and needs.
3. Choice about feedback on needs not met. Ask your partner or partners if they want to receive feedback about what you didn't like as much, what didn't meet your needs. Give them options for what they could do differently, what you would have preferred. Keep checking on whether they want to hear more. If you're receiving feedback, ask for the feedback you want, what you want to know about.

Dyad Practice Exercise: Shoe Feedback

1. Give your partner positive judgments about their shoes. For example, "Oh, those are so stylish."
2. Next, give your partner OFN "biofeedback" about the shoes:
   • The specific things about the shoes that you like
   • How you feel (in your body versus your thoughts) when you think of these things
   • The needs of yours that are met
3. Ask your partner if they want to hear what you don't like. Partner says yes. Give OFN feedback on needs not met (make it up if you want).
4. Ask your partner again if they want to hear what you don't like. This time, partner says no.
5. Tell each other which type of feedback you prefer, judgment- or needs-based, and why.

FLIGHT SIMULATOR: PRACTICE GUIDELINES

STARTING THE PRACTICE SESSION:

1. Brief check-in for each of you to say how you are, how your day is going.
2. See if someone has a real situation that they would like to "put into the chairs." If not, create a general context, such as a relationship, family, or workplace conflict. Then start improvising the role-play.
3. Decide which person's situation the group will focus on. (If you can't decide together, then that is the mediation to work with!)

SETTING UP THE ROLE-PLAY:

1. Person whose situation it is plays themselves; the two partners play the other person and the mediator.
2. Whoever offered the scenario shapes the role-play with one observation of what the person being role-played (by a volunteer from the group) said or did that was challenging. No need to tell the whole story.
3. Mediator dials the difficulty so as to remain in the learning zone:
   a) What skill do you want to focus on?
   b) How much intensity do you want in the role-playing?
4. Make an agreement with your coach, if you have one, regarding how you want them to coach.
5. Mediator performs self-empathy before starting the role-play (we recommend saying out loud your thoughts, feelings, and needs, and any requests of your self or others).
6. We recommend budgeting 10–15 minutes for mediating and 5–10 minutes for giving feedback at the end of each mediator's turn. Have a timekeeper.

DURING THE ROLE-PLAY (IN THE "FLIGHT SIMULATOR"):

1. Pause the role-play to do self-connection/self-empathy, silently or out loud.
2. Pause and consider out loud your options.
3. Pause and ask others for their feedback.
4. Ask your practice partners to dial the difficulty up or down.
5. Rewind and do over what you want to practice.
6. Observers and coach take notes, focusing as much or more on what you see that is meeting needs vs. what you see that is not meeting needs.

AFTER THE ROLE-PLAY (DEBRIEFING AND FEEDBACK; SEE PRACTICE AND FEEDBACK SECTION ABOVE):

1. Debriefing.
2. Feedback on needs met.
3. Ask if feedback about needs not met is welcome.
4. After feedback, rotate. The person who offered the scenario takes on the role of the "other," and, in the final rotation, the role of the mediator.
5. Give feedback to the coach regarding their coaching.

Chapter 4

Temporal Contexts of Mediation

Map: Enemy Image Process (EIP)

"Enemy image," a term borrowed from Marshall Rosenberg, refers to a cluster of judgments that forms in our mind around the image of another person, and that blocks us from actually seeing them.

This obviously makes it more challenging for us to feel a sense of connection with them or to feel care and compassion toward them. It prevents us from recognizing our common humanity. When we create negative images of others based in critical thoughts of them as wrong, bad, and perhaps deserving to be punished, we not only cut ourselves off from them, but also usually experience a lot of pain ourselves. We may feel bitterness, resentment, anger, or even hatred. As we hold these enemy images, we suffer, and we also become much less effective in responding to the person and the situation in skillful ways that are likely to meet our needs. Note that an enemy image can be created out of negative or positive judgments. We may, for instance, feel resentful when someone seems to exist on a pedestal or to somehow be a better human being than the rest of us.

We are also under the influence of our enemy images when we are around one of our cultural icons and become nervous, tongue tied, and generally ill at ease. In this case our judgments are positive, but these thoughts nonetheless disconnect us from this other person.

In formal mediation, we can use the Enemy Image Process (EIP) to prepare both ourselves and/or our clients to be more open and present in the midst of conflict. In our interactions with clients, we may form judgments and images of them. We may think,

"He is a bad person," or, "She will never change." Or we may think, "This person is so smart and understands so much more than I do." This can make it more difficult to contribute to the mediation process in the way we want, but we can use the EIP to work with our own enemy images. We can also have individual pre-mediation sessions with the parties to prepare each of them for the process, supporting both sides of the conflict by transforming their enemy images of each other.

Below we describe the basic application of the EIP, how to use it as part of a self-empathy process, and how to use it to translate our own judgments in preparation for a conversation.

THE ENEMY IMAGE PROCESS

1. Self-empathy. *Self*-connection with one's own experience and needs (OFN/observations, feelings, needs)
2. Empathy for other. *Self*-connection with other's experience and needs (OFN)
3. Emergence of new possibilities to meet needs (R/requests)
   a) **Learning.** Checking how we feel now about the situation. Have we shifted in regard to it? Do we have any new ideas?
   b) **Planning.** Is there anything I want to plan for the future?
   c) **Practice.** Do I want to practice something to prepare myself for the next interaction?

CYCLING

As you move to connecting with feelings and needs, you may notice more judgments and reactions. If so, cycle, or loop, between observing your thoughts and connecting with feelings and needs. As you move toward empathizing with the other's needs, you may get triggered

NOTES

into more judgments and emotional reactions. If this happens, cycle back to part 1 until you feel reconnected to your needs, then try coming back to part 2, empathy for others. Cycle back and forth as needed. This cycling can also happen between parts 1, 2, and 3.

DOING THE ENEMY IMAGE PROCESS

Step 1. Empathy for Yourself (OFN)

a) Observations. Name what you are observing in yourself.

- Identify what happened, the facts, simply describing the behavior.
- Describe your thoughts, judgments, evaluations, and demands regarding how things should or should not be, what's right or wrong, good or bad. What thoughts do you observe going through your mind as you think about that event in the present? Be as free-flowing and uncensored as you can with this.

b) Feelings. Name what you are feeling in your body (vs. your thinking).

- How are you feeling as you think about the event now (rather than how you were feeling when it happened)?
- Be mindful of using faux-feeling language that refers to your thinking rather than the feelings, sensations, and emotions alive inside you. Use the feelings list if that's helpful.
- Also, we suggest that you give yourself some time and quiet space to really feel how you are feeling, to really experience being in your body awareness, rather than only mentally labeling the feeling.

c) Needs. What needs of yours around this are not met?

- Identify what needs you connect with in

NOTES

relation to what the other person said or did and your thoughts and feelings. What words or phrases for needs most deeply and satisfyingly resonate with you?

- Be mindful of using language that mixes universal needs with specific strategies. Use the needs list if it's helpful.

- Again, we suggest that you take the space to really feel what's happening in your body as you search for the words that best resonate with you, until you notice a "shift" quality in your body—a feeling of opening, relaxation, softening, peace, compassion, and connection with yourself and others.

- Once you have found some language for your needs, try savoring and deepening your connection to them, enjoying and appreciating their significance to you and the richness they bring.

Step 2. Empathy for the other person (OFN)
  **a) Imagine possible needs motivating the
    other person.**

- What needs might the other person be trying to meet for themselves when they act in that manner? (That is, in the manner that you have judged them to be acting in.) Use the needs list for help if you want.

- Do not worry about your accuracy. The purpose as we see it is not to know what their needs are, but rather to create connection and compassion within yourself by putting your attention on needs of theirs that you as a human being can relate to.

- Continue imagining and wondering until you feel some kind of bodily shift to connection and compassion. You may need to periodically go back and reconnect with your needs not met in this situation.

b) Imagine what the other person might be perceiving, thinking, and feeling

- It may be helpful to you to guess the perceptions, thoughts, and feelings that are going on in the other when they do what they do.
- Use the feelings list if it is helpful to you.

Step 3: Learn, Plan, Practice

- See if you have a specific, doable (what you want, rather than what you don't want), action-language request or requests of yourself or someone. What can you or they do to contribute to your meeting needs (your needs to care for yourself and your needs to care for others)?
- Rather than trying to figure it out or working at it in any way, see whether, in putting your attention on your needs and connecting with them, a request arises spontaneously in your awareness.
- You may also want to plan and practice what you might actually say to this person in a conversation and how they might respond, and then how you might respond to their response, and so on.

Another possibility is to ask someone to role-play with you to further plan and practice for the conversation.

NOTES

CASE STUDY: ENEMY IMAGE PROCESS

Here's an example of how a mediator might use the EIP on himself.

I am coming home from another mediation with a couple. In thinking about the next session we have planned, I reflect on my enemy image of the woman, which I know will interfere with my connection with her. During the mediation, the woman had said to her partner, "You will never do enough. You should try harder, but I might never forgive you anyway." I notice discomfort and judgmental thoughts about my clients and myself, so I decide to do the Enemy Image Process.

Step 1:
My thoughts go something like this: "I can't stand it anymore. How can she talk to her husband like that? She is the reason they will never reconnect, because she blames him. And I will never be able to support them. It is beyond my skills. This conflict is too deep for my skills."

I am feeling hopeless and desperate and would like to trust that I can be present. I am so sad and frustrated when I hear the words they are using in this conversation. I want respect and care for everyone in the room. Also, I would like to have trust in change. I want to trust in my skills and experience and trust that I can support them. I also notice that I want to do my best and be able to let go of the outcome of this conversation, or to lightly hold responsibility for the outcome and share that responsibility with the people involved in this mediation.

Step 2:
Being more clear about my needs and as a result feeling more connected with myself, I notice I am curious about what is going on for my clients, especially for the woman. She said, "You will never do enough. You should try harder, but I might never forgive you anyway." I am guessing she might be feeling desperate and wanting healing around the events of the past. She might be wanting empathy, to be heard and understood, but at the same time wanting to trust that it will bring relief for her. She might also be torn, wanting to be honest about both how painful her experience is right now and how doubtful she is about the whole mediation process.

Step 3:

Having more peace in myself about this conversation, I realize I need support in this mediation. It occurs to me to ask my triad practice group next week to role-play this mediation, so I can gain more understanding and get some more ideas about how best to support this couple.

ROLE-PLAYING THE ENEMY IMAGE PROCESS

Another way to use the EIP map is in a role-play with a practice partner or a client. You can use this role-play when you are the one who has the enemy image and also when you are supporting another person to transform his. In a formal mediation, this can be useful if you are in a pre-mediation session with one of the disputants or if you are in the role of a coach.

Step 1:
- Use the same three EIP steps from p. 4.2.
- Imagine you are in the role of the coach and the person you are working with is the client. Imagine that your client has the enemy images and she or he has asked you for support and you have agreed together to do an EIP role-play.
- In the first step of the role-play, the client gives voice to any judgmental thoughts about the other person; i.e., the enemy images held of that person. Many of these thoughts may be embarrassing or shameful for the client to acknowledge. The client may need empathy from you as the coach before being willing to say them out loud. The client may also welcome an agreement that you will forget the judgmental thoughts and to only remember those thoughts as they are transformed into unmet needs. Within each of those judgmental thoughts is a heartwarming and uplifting need. In this safe space, encourage the client to let judgmental thoughts out by giving them voice. (Marshall Rosenberg called this "letting the jackals out to play," and the jackals are a metaphor for language that disconnects us from ourselves and others.)
- As the coach, first play the role of the other — the person about whom the client has enemy images. In the role of the other, empathize with the client, who is playing himself or herself. Your goal is to help the client identify the needs that underlie each of the judgments s/he has about the other person. To get there, you may find it helpful to identify the observations connected to the judgments, the feelings that arise while thinking about each judgment, and then the un-met needs which the judgments are seeking to express.

- Continue until the client is complete. Ensure each enemy image has been translated into needs, and there is nothing the first person wants to say, as of that time, about the other person.
- Switch chairs.

Step 2:

- The client now plays the other person in the role-play. As coach, you now take on the role of your client.
- Your client now gives voice to all the judgments the client imagines the other has about the client. The client speaks in the first person as if they were the other person, and says all the things about the client that the client has heard the other person say to them, or presumes the other may have said to others, or suspects the other may be thinking.
- Listen to what is said and empathize with what your client is saying in the role of the other. Stay with this until the client is complete.

Step 3: (Learn, Plan, Practice)

- Learn — When you have some sense your client is complete, invite her or him to reflect upon the process. You can do this by asking questions like:

   "How was that for you?"

   "Do you feel a difference between when we started this process and now?"

   "What have you learned by doing this process?"

- Plan — After reflecting upon what they have learned, clients typically will start talking about what they want to do about the situation they are in with the other person. This demonstrates that the process has given them a new way of looking at the world. As coach, you are now in a position to use your skills to help the client make Solutions Requests (see p. 3.32) of himself or herself, so s/he can make plans. Plans are, after all, a series of requests that clients make of themselves.

LEARNING CYCLE (SMALL CYCLE)

When learning from something that happened between ourselves and another, shifting the focus to meeting needs changes how we are in the world. Most of us have been taught by our cultures how to avoid punishment and blame as opposed to how to meet our individual needs. The impulses to avoid punishment and to meet our needs can be thought of as two learning cycles, or feedback loops.

The learning cycle that most of us received from our childhood training follows a predictable pattern. First, we do something. Then, we and others around us analyze, diagnose, and judge whether we should be praised, blamed, or punished. The implicit message is to avoid blame and punishment at all costs.

NVC provides an alternative learning cycle. First, we do something. Next, we and others assess whether this action met our needs and others' needs. Finally, we learn from this how to better meet needs in the future. Below is a diagram of the positive feedback loop. It's represented as a spiral because, although each trip around the loop again brings us to something we are doing, we do not come around to the same place as before, but rather to a new place created out of our learning.

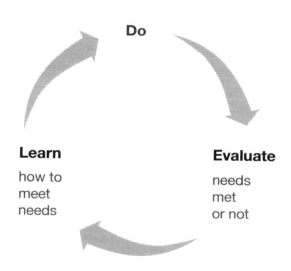

Do

Learn
how to
meet
needs

Evaluate
needs
met
or not

Map: Mourn/Celebrate/Learn (MCL)

Whether we are doing work on ourselves or supporting others, we think of a challenging conversation with another person as having two bookends. We typically use the Enemy Image Process (EIP) to prepare for the coming interaction. Afterward, we generally use the three-part mourn/celebrate/learn (MCL) process to look back at and evaluate what happened.

In reflecting on the conversation, we notice our thoughts or feelings about what happened and what we and others did. Because we often first go to our judgments of blame and criticism, we first identify the needs that were not met and mourn those. Second, we celebrate, looking for the things we or others said or did in the conversation that we liked and identifying needs that were met. We can also celebrate needs that we or others were trying to meet, even if unsuccessfully, and we can also imagine what needs might be met in the future from this happening as it did. Third, we *learn* from the whole process and make a plan for how we will try to better meet our needs in the future.

MCL is a powerful process that supports us to step out of judgments about what happened, what we did, or what someone else did, and step into a world focused on meeting our own needs and the needs of those around us. We can also use it to care for ourselves after mediation or any experience that brings up intrusive judgmental thoughts of ourselves or our choices. In applying the MCL process, we learn from our conversations and determine the next action we want to take to try to meet needs.

MOURN/CELEBRATE/LEARN (MCL)

A key component of this process is a cycling between parts 1, 2, and 3.

1. **Mourn**—We notice our thoughts and feelings about the situation and inquire into the needs not met by what we did and what happened.

2. **Celebrate**—We notice what we did or what happened that we liked, and inquire into and appreciate the needs we met or tried to meet

3. **Learn** from what happened (new strategies for more effectively meeting needs).

   a) Learn—With what I know now, how might I have done things differently in the situation ("post-hearsal")?

   b) Plan—Is there anything I want to plan for the future?

   c) Practice—Do I want to practice something to prepare myself to be able to do what I would like to do?

CASE STUDY: MCL PROCESS

Here's an example of how a mediator might use the MCL process on herself.

After a difficult phone conversation with mediation clients I feel generally upset. As I begin to pay attention to this, I notice that I am thinking, "I am terrible at this," and, "I should not continue working as a mediator." When I bring to the center of my consciousness that I am having these thoughts, I notice that my general sense of upset coalesces into feeling frustrated, hurt, and disappointed. I ask myself what needs of mine are not being met if I am feeling this way. I begin to realize that I am feeling frustrated because my need to contribute is not being met in ways that I like.

NOTES

I remember now that during the conversation I asked one person whether he had a need for respect and consideration, and he replied with irritation in his voice, "No, no, it is not respect, for sure." From that moment on I felt some distance between us that lasted until the end of the conversation. I realize that it was my judgment that created my discomfort.

I am feeling hurt because I wanted to have a sense of connection with the person I was speaking with on the phone, and my efforts at connection were not received as I had hoped. Also I am feeling disappointed because I had hoped for a certain kind of connection and contribution, which did not seem to happen.

As I become connected with the needs that I did want to meet and that were not met, how I feel changes. I begin to feel more sad than frustrated, hurt, or disappointed. The sadness is more in line with my regret and mourning—the grieving I am doing over the lost opportunity to have the connection and contribution that I had hoped for.

Doing this portion of the MCL process is satisfying and relieving. Yet I remember the possibility of the second step of the MCL process, which is to celebrate the needs I did meet or that at least I had hoped to meet. As soon as I remember this second step, I inquire of myself, "What needs of mine were met, either by what I did or by what the other person did?" What pops to mind right away is that my need for contribution was met in part. I do appreciate my intention of support that I would like to see for all people when in conflict with others. So, I am gratified at my attempts, my efforts, to create the kind of support that I want us all to have. I realize that I am also celebrating specific moments in the conversation when I tried some of the things I have been learning. I feel really good that I tried them. I realize that for the most part I feel good about how I did what I did. For example, I liked the way I interrupted with self-expression at the very beginning of the conversation.

I also now remember that several times during the conversation, I noticed I was triggered when they talked over each other. In the past I might have been prompted by this to say something that I regretted later. This time, I was able to notice that I was triggered, reconnect with myself, and make a different choice that now I can reflect upon and learn.

This brings me to the third phase of the MCL process, the learning phase. I reflect upon what I have learned by mourning and celebrating. I realize that although there is much I do not like about how the interaction went, I am also pleased about some of the things

I did do. In considering both my mourning and celebrating, I conclude that I do not see anything I would like to say differently in the mediation next time. However, I would like to be able to respond differently internally. To do that, I know I need to practice, so I plan to role-play this example with my dyad partner and practice self-empathy after hearing, "No, no, it is not respect, for sure."

LEARNING CYCLE (LARGER CYCLE)

Similar to the learning cycle described as part of the mourn/celebrate/learn process (MCL) is a learning cycle that goes from preparing oneself or another for a conflict conversation with the Enemy Image Process, then having the conversation, and then learning from what happened in that conversation with the MCL. And the learning that comes out of the MCL can then lead into another preparation for another conversation. This too can be thought of as a spiral. Each time around we are in a different place because of the learning and growth from working with these processes. In this sense there is never failure. There is simply doing, learning, and preparing for another doing.

PRE- AND POST-MEDIATION

Pre-mediation sessions are an opportunity to do the Enemy Image Process (EIP) with disputants prior to the mediation session, in a one-on-one telephone call or in-person session. This is also a time to let them know what to expect and to answer their questions. When the disputant who contacts you is also the one who engages you, the pre-mediation session and the engagement call may take place at the same time. Even in these instances, you might schedule a separate pre-mediation call.

You might use the EIP to track where you are.

Post-mediation practices that apply to you as the mediator are discussed below in the section "Mediator Self-Care." Also, sometimes you may find yourself with one or more of the disputants after the mediation session. You may contact them for feedback or as part of completing an agreement during the session. One of the disputants may also contact you, for similar reasons.

The challenge here is to support people to return to connection with self and other(s) so that they can move into the learning cycle and prepare for the next step(s).

The mourn/celebrate/learn (MCL) cycle occurs after an event such as a mediation. The person you are with may want to celebrate parts that met their needs and mourn parts that did not. This celebrating and mourning shifts us out of our socially conditioned judgments about ourselves and others and into learning how better to meet needs.

MEDIATOR SELF-CARE

Self-care means using the Mediate Your Life approach to take care of ourselves when we are in distress, and also to celebrate when our needs are met. Mediator self-care consists of working with our own judgments of and reactions to the disputants before, during, and after the mediation.

It makes sense to take ourselves as mediators through the EIP and the MCL. We may enlist a colleague to support us in doing this. Asking for help is one of the most underutilized skills for self-care.

More information on mediator self-care appears in John and Ike's article, "Becoming a Better Mediator by Mediating Your Internal Dialogue." (See Chapter 8, "Resources.")

Chapter 5

Other Maps of the Integral Grid

Map: Interpersonal Mediation Model (IPM)

Sometimes you face the challenge of applying the mediation skills and process when you are a disputant in an interpersonal mediation context. Thus, you have two roles. Seeking to facilitate connected communication while swept up in the dynamics of the conflict can present obvious challenges.

INTERPERSONAL MEDIATION MODEL

1. SCP
2. Ask yourself, "Can I hear the message as a 'please'?"
   a. "Please" = "I have an unmet need and a request"
   b. "Thank you" = "I'm grateful for a need of mine that was met"
3. Focus empathy toward the Other (if you have the capacity)
   a. Empathy for other (silent or out loud)
   b. Self-expression
4. Focus empathy toward yourself (self-expression and connection requests)
5. Solution Requests and Agreements
   a. Present-tense, positive, in action language (specificity)

NOTES

Map: 4-Step Healing and Reconciliation Model

NVC founder Marshall Rosenberg developed the 4-Step Healing and Reconciliation (H&R) model to address past emotional hurt.

In much of what we do using the Mediate Your Life approach, whether it's in coaching or pre-mediation or mediation sessions, there is an aspect of emotional healing, of reconciliation both internally and with others. One aspect of conflict is a clash of beliefs and strategies for meeting needs. Another aspect is the stimulation of emotional hurt and pain. Often both parties in a conflict feel emotionally injured in relation to the other's actions. Sometimes both parties agree that one of them was the "author" of an action that stimulated hurt for the other, the "receiver" of that action. Dominic Bartner coined the terms author and receiver in his Restorative Circles work.

THE FOUR STEPS OF THE HEALING & RECONCILIATION MODEL ARE:

NOTES

1. **Empathy:** "Receiver" expresses and the "Actor" who stimulated emotional hurt or pain gives Empathy to Receiver.

2. **Mourning:** Actor expresses "Mourning" to Receiver

3. **Understanding:** Actor expresses the needs they were trying to meet when they did what they did. The Actor does this in order to meet the Receiver's need for Understanding, but only if the Receiver expresses a desire to hear this.

4. **Healing and Restorative actions:** Together, the Actor and Receiver search for requests or actions to further contribute to Healing and Reconciliation. Actor agrees to use more effective, less costly ways of meeting their needs in the future.

MORE EXPLANATION OF THE FOUR STEPS OF THE HEALING & RECONCILIATION MODEL: HOW TO FACILITATE EACH STEP

Step 1: Empathy

Actor empathizes with Receiver (using the 4 elements of empathy)

  a) Receiver expresses their hurt and pain to the Actor,

  b) Actor stays in empathy until Receiver says they've said all that they want to say. Actor may want to ask the Receiver multiple times if there is anything else they want to say, and if they feel heard and understood as they would like. If they show hesitation, we recommend staying with Step I.

  For example, Actor asks: *"Is there more you want me to hear?"*

Step 2: Mourning

Actor expresses mourning to the Receiver

  a) Actor asks something like, *"Would you like to hear what comes up in me hearing what you are saying?"*

  b) Actor expresses sincere sadness, regret, etc. Here are examples of three types of mourning we have identified:

  i. "When I see your pain, I feel sad."

  ii. "When I see how what I did has affected you, I feel sad."

  iii. "Seeing the impact on you, I see how it doesn't meet my own values, and I'm sad about that."

  c) Actor ends each expression of mourning by making a connection request like *"How do you feel hearing this?"*

  If the Receiver responds with an expression of pain, go back to step 1 and empathize with the Receiver

Step 3: Understanding

Actor expresses the needs they were trying to meet. The purpose and intent of this step is for the Actor to meet the Receiver's need for understanding.

  a) Actor asks something like, *"Would you like to hear what was going on in me when I did what I did?"*

  i. If Receiver says "no" or seems in any way hesitant, then go back to Steps 1 and 2, or proceed to Step 4.

  ii. If Receiver says "yes," then Actor expresses the needs they were trying to meet when they did what they did.

b) After each expression of the needs they were trying to meet, the Actor may want to combine this with mourning.

For example, *"When I did what I did, I believe I was meeting the need for ____ , and I'm so sad I did it in a way that was distressing to you."*

c) After each expression of the needs they were trying to meet, the Actor may want to make a connection request that checks the Receiver's understanding of what they heard the Actor say.

For example, *"Would you tell me what you heard me say, so I know you heard me the way I want?"*

Step 4: Healing and Restorative Actions

Actor and Receiver search together for restorative or healing actions

a) Make requests for specific actions to further healing and compassionate giving and receiving.

For example, Receiver might ask something like, *"Would you tell me how I matter to you?" "Would you tell me what I could do to help restore our relationship?"* or *"Are you willing to brainstorm how we might learn from this for the future?"*

b) Find more effective, less costly ways for Actor to get needs met.

For example, the Actor might say something like, *"If in the future I am hurt or angry with you, I will come and talk directly with you about it. Does that work for you?"*

THE HEALING & RECONCILIATION 4-STEP MODEL CAN BE USED IN AT LEAST FIVE WAYS:

1. Making Amends: When you are perceived as the Actor in another's hurt and you want to restore your relationship with this person, you can use the 4-Steps of the Healing and Reconciliation Model to attempt to make amends. Typically, in a situation where you would want to make amends, you too are in pain about what has taken place. If you carry this pain into the conversation with the other person, you will probably not be able to effectively use the Making Amends map. Therefore, we find it essential for the Actor to first get their own needs for empathy met through their own internal processes or with support from another person. With your own need for empathy met, you will then be able to listen empathically to the Receiver, without the Receiver triggering your own pain. You will also be able to empathize with them in a way that creates connection and healing.

2. Healing Role-Play: When you are the Receiver and you're working with a practice partner to have relief from your pain, you can ask your practice partner to play the role of the Actor. In this role, the practice partner does not try to play the role like the "real" Actor might. Instead, the practice partner utilizes all the skills they have to go through the 4-Steps of the Healing and Reconciliation Model as if they were Making Amends to you. Your task in this role play is to play yourself. In Step 1, express your pain with as little editing as possible. In order to do this, it's helpful to be with a practice partner you trust will not judge you for your condemnations of the Actor.

3. Practice Role-Play for Making Amends: When you want to prepare to make amends with someone, you can practice by role playing the process with you playing the Actor and your practice partner playing the Receiver. You can use all the tools of the Flight Simulator to pause in order to self-connect, get feedback from your practice partner, dial up or down the difficulty and identify and try alternative ways of communicating. In many ways, doing this is similar to the Intensity Exercise, in which you have the support to reconnect and desensitize yourself to triggers delivered by your practice partner.

4. Mediating Healing and Reconciliation Between Others: The Healing and Reconciliation Model can be used when you are facilitating a conversation between two people, at least one of whom perceives themselves to have been hurt by the other person in the conversation. Thus, at least one of the two parties perceive themselves as the Receiver and the other as the Actor. Most often in these situations, both parties perceive themselves as the Receiver and the other as the Actor. In the latter case, you will need to obtain agreement as to who first plays the role of the Receiver. Alternatively, you can agree to caucus with each of the parties that perceive themselves as the Receiver and do the Healing Role-Play with them.

Only use the Healing and Reconciliation model in a mediation context when you have obtained agreement from the parties to do so. In order to do this process with the real Actor and Receiver, you generally need to be very directive in your facilitation. By being "directive," we in part mean to be willing to interrupt the parties in order request that they stay within the four steps of the model.

People rarely come in asking for healing and reconciliation; they come in wanting specific agreements with the other party about a certain situation. However, particularly when the relationship is long-standing, harbored hurt may stand in the way of getting to that agreement. When preparing for a mediation, you may get the sense that old pain on one side or the other will limit the movement towards connection and resolution between the parties. You can surface this pain by letting them know that in your experience, until they work through this hurt, they are less likely to be able to get to the result they have said they want.

Before going into the process, make sure both the Actor and the Receiver are in agreement about their roles and the action that was taken by the Actor.

5. Checklist in Mediation: Integrating the Healing and Reconciliation Model with the 5-Step Mediation Model When you are using the 5-Step Mediation Model to mediate between two or more people who have been hurt by the other, you can have an internal checklist that tracks the four steps of the Healing and Reconciliation Model for each of the parties.

Dyad/Triad Practice Exercise: Healing and Reconciliation

For a dyad exercise, one person plays the author (the person whose conduct is the subject of the reconciliation process) and the other plays the receiver (the person who feels like the victim or wronged party). For a triad exercise, a third person plays the mediator. A dyad exercise is outlined here.

1. The author empathizes with the pain of the receiver.
2. When it is clear that the receiver has had his need for empathy met, shift to mourning the

needs of the author, which are not met when she takes in the consequences of her actions on the person who thinks of himself as the victim.

3. Note that the receiver will often ask why the author did what she did. One way to think of this is that the receiver is trying to understand why something happened to him. He wants an explanation that makes sense. The author tries to provide that understanding by explaining what needs she was trying to meet when she did what the receiver is distressed about.

4. In the final phase, the dyad or triad works to propose actions intended to heal and restore connection and community.

INNER MEDIATION CONTEXT

We can apply the mediation skills and process to our own self-judgments. This is mediation between different parts of ourselves—between the warring voices in our heads. There are two maps for inner mediation: the internal mediation model and the chooser-educator process. It can be very powerful to take a conflict we're experiencing with another and see if we can find a corresponding self-judgment in which different parts of ourselves are at odds.

Map: Internal Mediation Model (IM)

One map of inner mediation is the internal mediation model (IM). The IM model is used when the conflict involves inner turmoil about the present or the future. This process applies the 5-step mediation model to different voices within us—empathizing with each, inviting them to hear each other, and then seeing what solution emerges. IM can also be powerful in "shadow work," in which we discover and work with parts of ourselves that strongly influence our behavior.

You can learn and practice this map by putting the voices in your head "into the chairs." This means to set up a role-play in which you give the disputants the words that are swirling through your head. The disputants then play the roles based on what they would do and how they would react if they were having thoughts like that. With time, you can learn to readily mediate the conversations in your head without putting the voices "into the chairs."

IM steps:

1. Empathize with the first voice that wants to be heard (Voice A)

Ask what voice wants to be heard first, and empathize with that voice (Voice A), using the four elements of empathy. Reflect back your understanding and get to the feelings and needs. It can help to ask this voice what its name is, and the role or function it is playing. You can think of this as akin to being in a dark room, and needing to ask questions to find out who's there. In shadow work, Voice A speaks about reactions to the external other.

2. Empathize with the second voice that wants to be heard (Voice B)

Ask what other voice wants to speak and be heard in relation to what Voice A has said. Empathize with that voice (Voice B), using the four elements of empathy. Reflect back your understanding as well as getting to the feelings and needs. You can ask this voice too about its name, role, function, etc.

- Sometimes other parts or aspects of the self emerge to be heard. If this happens empathize with each.
- When using IM for shadow work, have the external person with whom there is conflict become an inner part or aspect of the self (Voice B), and empathize with this voice. Another option is to look for some other part or parts of the self that are somehow related to the person or the pattern or dynamic in the external conflict.

3. Ask Voice B to empathize with Voice A.

Ask Voice B if it would say to Voice A what it heard A say and its needs.

4. Ask Voice A to empathize with Voice B.

Ask Voice A if it would say to Voice B what it heard B say and its needs.

- If there have been more than two voices speaking, then ask the ones in conflict with each other to reflect back what they heard each other say and their needs.

[Cycle through steps 1-4 as need to create inner understanding and connection.]

NOTES

5. Solution Requests.

Ask Voice B if it has any requests for how to meet both of their needs. Ask Voice A if it has any requests. Continue and see if you can reach inner clarity about what to do.

> # Map: Chooser-Educator Process (C-E)

Chooser-Educator (C-E) process is one of the inner mediation maps for navigating conflicts between different parts or aspects of ourselves, when we are evaluating ourselves negatively after we have taken an action in the past (i.e., through a conscious or unconscious choice).

CHOOSER-EDUCATOR PROCESS

1. Empathy with the inner "Educator" (the voice of self-evaluation/judgment)

Listen to what the voice of the Educator is saying, and empathize with it, using the four elements of empathy. Reflect back your understanding and get to the feelings and needs of the Educator. The Educator is expressing, or communicating about, needs not met by the action or actions of the Chooser. The Educator may express its needs through the language of moralistic self-judgments, "stories," demands – language stating or implying wrongness, badness, "should have," criticism, blame, or punishment. The emotion that tends to come from the Educator is anger, with fear underneath. By transforming the language of the Educator into a language of needs, there is a shift from self-blame to "mourning," natural feelings of sadness and regret.

2. Empathy with the inner "Chooser" (the part of ourselves that did or chose what the Educator is evaluating)

Ask the inner "Chooser" to say what it wants to be heard about, and empathize with it, using the four elements of empathy. You could ask how the Chooser feels about how the Educator is talking to it. Often the emotions that come from the Chooser are guilt, shame, and anxiety, but also sometimes anger towards the Educator. You can then ask what needs the Chooser was trying to meet when it did what it did. The Chooser used a particular strategy to meet a need or needs. Empathy for the Chooser is understanding how that strategy was the best the Chooser knew to do at the time to meet the needs it was trying to meet. This understanding brings self-compassion. And even if the strategy was not successful, there can be an appreciation, or even celebration, for how the Chooser was trying to meet needs.

3. Ask the Chooser to empathize with the Educator. Ask the Chooser if it would say to the Educator what it heard the Educator say and its needs.

4. Ask the Educator to empathize with the Chooser. Ask the Educator if it would say to the Chooser what it heard the Chooser say and its needs.

[Cycle through steps 1-4 as need to create inner understanding and connection.]

5. Solution Requests. Ask the Educator if it has any requests for how to meet both of their needs. Ask the Chooser if it has requests. One way to gain clarity on this is to look back and imagine other ways of responding, new possibilities. See if you can reach an inner agreement.

LENDING MEDIATION SKILLS IN GROUPS

Mediating in groups makes the tracking process of the 5-step mediation model more complex, but the inherent structure is the same. You can mediate in groups formally or informally. There is a map for the understanding and connection phase (group mediation model) and also one for the emergent solutions phase (group decision making).

For more about conflict resolution in groups, see the article "Group Decision Making: A Nonviolent Communication Perspective," by Ike Lasater with Julie Stiles.

ACCRETED MEDIATION

Accreted mediation in groups often involves:

- Adding one conversation to the next, seeing what emerges as the next step is taken. The mediation consists of the series of conversations that do not necessarily include a joint session with all the disputants.
- Bringing together smaller to larger subgroupings, working up to mediating with the whole group.

For more on accreted mediation, see the article "Accreted Mediation: Building Clarity and Connection," by Ike Lasater with Julie Stiles, at http://www.mediate.com/articles/lasaterstiles2.cfm.

Map: Group Mediation Model

1. Who wants to speak now?
2. Empathize with speaker, getting to needs.
3. Ask if speaker would like someone in the group to reflect back what they said, and if so, whom they would like to do this. Mediator might have a request or suggestion about someone reflecting and who this would be.
4. If someone reflects, support the person to do this.
5. Group decision-making process for facilitating solution requests and agreements.

Map: Group Decision-Making Process (GDM)

FORMAL GDM PROCESS

The group version of the "need behind the no" process of the emergent solutions phase.
1. After gathering the needs to be met and brainstorming creative ideas, ask who wants to make a solution request.
2. Help speaker clarify their request or proposal and connect it to needs.

3. Ask group if anyone's needs were not met by the proposal and empathize with each person who in some way says no, getting to the needs keeping them from saying yes.

4. Ask if anyone in the group has a new solution request or proposal to meet all the needs. Empathize with each person who says no, and ask that person if they have a new request that will meet all the needs.

INFORMAL GDM PROCESS

For when we don't have a formal role of mediator or facilitator of the group conversation.

1. Do self-connection practice if triggered by what's happening in the group.

2. Is the speaker saying "please" or "thank you"?

3. Help person get clear on their needs and their request of the group.

4. Empathize with any "no" from other group members.

5. Help other group members get clear their requests to meet all the needs expressed.

NOTES

Chapter 6

Professional Development

THE ENGAGEMENT CONVERSATION MODEL

The engagement conversation model is a framework for for conversations that might lead to employment, particularly when we are asked what we do in social settings and when people call to inquire about our services.

The three steps of this model are:
1. **Connection:** This is the initial part of the conversation that is often dealt with by saying "Hello. How are you?" The goal is connection.
2. **Mutual Education:** This is a more free form step in which you seek to learn what the potential client wants and it is a time for you to demonstrate your communication skills and to describe what services you're offering.
3. **Agreements:** This is the phase in which you agree to next steps, which may be as straightforward as scheduling a further conversation or agreeing to send information.

Speaking to someone who is interested in engaging our services is an opportunity for connection. Out of that connection can grow a relationship that we feel good about. This may lead to our being employed by the person. Whether it does or not, we will have greatly increased the likelihood that the person will speak favorably of us to others. This is one of the central mechanisms of word-of-mouth outreach. The other central piece of word-of-mouth outreach is providing services that others are pleased about. This is covered below.

The engagement conversation is an opportunity for the caller to experience the essence of what we have to offer: an empathic understanding of self and others that leads to connection. Interestingly, you can also use the Enemy Image Process in the mutual education step of the Engagement Conversation.

Typically, when someone calls for mediation services, they welcome questions along the lines of, "Would you tell me what's going on?" As they respond to this question, we can shift into hearing and reflecting their observations, feelings, needs, and requests. So, in effect, we are now in the first phase of the Enemy Image Process. As this is happening, we are also gaining the information we need to assess what we might enjoy doing to support them.

As their need for empathy for their situation begins to be met, they will often signal a shift to focusing on the other person or persons in the conflict. This then opens a possibility of shifting to the second phase of the Enemy Image Process, which may sound something like this: "When you say this person is impossible, what are they saying or doing that prompts you to say or do that?" With this question, we are looking for observations.

The third phase of the Enemy Image Process during an engagement conversation might consist of reviewing what has gone on during the call and any increased clarity that the caller has experienced. This might be the time to answer any remaining questions about our services and to educate about what you do. And now that you have this empathic understanding, you are particularly well prepared to tell the person what you would be confident doing for them.

The engagement conversation thus has an aspect of coaching and sometimes also has the feel of an interpersonal mediation. As such, *it can be practiced.* There's a flow and a rhythm of, first, empathy for the person you are speaking with; second, empathy for the others in the conflict; and third, learning from the first two phases and learning what to do next.

PROFESSIONAL SUSTAINABILITY

Outreach and talking about money are also learnable skills. When we notice discomfort or distress about activities pertaining to the business side of our work, we can put these conversations "into the chairs" or connect in other ways with the needs from which the distress is arising.

CONFLICT COACHING

Conflict coaching involves the challenge of supporting those who are in conflict with one or more people when there is no agreement to use a mediator. Conflict coaching and pre-mediation sessions are similar, the major difference being that, when acting as a coach, we are not anticipating engaging in the role of mediator. We are supporting the person we are coaching to:

- Clarify their own needs related to the conflict
- Guess the needs of the other parties
- Plan what strategies they would like to use
- Practice communication aspects of their plan

Often, but not always, coaching will extend over several sessions organized to precede and follow a difficult conversation that the "coachee" is anticipating. The pre-session is used to prepare and the post-session is used to mourn/celebrate/learn and practice. The practice here may consist of us role-playing with the coachee or the other party, often to prepare for the next anticipated difficult conversation. After the initial coaching session, subsequent sessions involve both reviewing what happened and what is anticipated to happen.

The coaching session itself might consist primarily of a role-play. The following is an example of a three-stage role-play that might take place in a coaching session: In the first stage, the coachee plays himself, and we as coach play the other person or persons in the conflict. We encourage the coachee to vent, and we meet this venting with empathic guesses. In this process, the coachee's need for empathy is met.

In the second stage, we switch roles, and the coachee says what he has heard the other person in the conflict say or what he imagines the other person's conflicts are. Again, we as the coach respond with empathic guessing. This provides the coachee with understanding of what the other person's needs might be.

In the third stage, we go back to the original configuration of the coachee playing himself and us playing the other person in the conflict. This is the practice phase. We agree with the coachee on what he would consider a manageable challenge. Then, playing the role of the other person, we deliver a hard-to-hear message to the coachee and use our support skills to help the coachee to reconnect with his own needs (return to presence) and craft a response that is in alignment with his values.

PUTTING BARRIERS IN THE CHAIRS

The skills described this manual and taught in our trainings revolve around mediating conflict. Ironically, one of the key situations in which conflict can arise is when you are seeking to reach a large life goal. As you take the steps to reach your goal, inevitably gaps will emerge between what you say you want to do and your emotional reaction to it. This signals that you've uncovered a barrier to what you want. Such barriers generally show up as run-of-the-mill internal conflicts, with part of you wanting to take the next step, and part of you holding back. You can put this barrier, this internal conflict, into the chairs with a practice partner and get support to mediate those internal voices.

Putting the barriers in the chairs helps you take the actions you want to take to reach your goals, and take them in a way that keeps you connected to your needs.

For example, let's say you have decided that you want to use the skills and capacities you have learned in the context of mediating conflicts and coaching others. Your goal is to build a sustainable business doing this work that you highly value. You first use your skills to be clear about what you want, going through the process of empathy, clarifying your needs and the strategies that you would like to meet them. This helps you get down to the specifics of a plan, and to lay out the concrete steps that you intend to take to build your business.

One of your next steps is to attend a networking event where you will have the opportunity to say a few words to the group about the services you offer as a mediator and conflict coach. Perhaps you find that in thinking about the event and what you might say, you feel heaviness throughout your body and your stomach feels hollow. You notice that a voice in your mind is saying; *"What am I thinking? What could I possibly say that would resonate with people? No one would want to come to me anyway. I should just skip it."* The two internal voices in conflict are the part of you that wants to do the event to market your services so you can build your business, and the part of you saying "Yes, but..." Use the internal mediation dyad practice with a partner to mediate this conflict and seek the resolution that supports you to reach your goals.

To put the barriers in the chairs:

1. Think about an action you want to take.
2. Notice how you feel.
3. Notice what additional thoughts follow.
4. Use this information to identify the two parts of you in conflict.
5. Put these internal voices in the chairs with your practice partner.

To support you as you build your business, you can, of course, take other processes from this manual into your dyad or triad practice sessions. After you go to the networking event, you could use the Mourn/Celebrate/Learn process to assess what happened. Prior to the event, you might also use the EIP if you are reluctant to talk to someone because you have judgments about that person.

NOTES

Chapter 7

Practicing Toward Your Goals

POST-INTENSIVE PRACTICE REQUESTS

> **"** We do not rise to the level of our expectations. We fall to the level of our training."
>
> —*Archilochus, Greek soldier and poet, c. 650 BC*

We refer often to the quotation above because it applies directly to how our participants learn in our immersion training programs. The skills and processes covered by the Mediate Your Life approach are not easily internalized without practice. The more consistent your practice, the more you will see positive changes in your habits and choices. Many of our participants have confirmed for us that the practice sessions in-between intensives are vitally important to reinforcing the work they do during the intensive retreats. Most people also report looking forward to the mutual support and empathy that are part of each practice group.

Our three practice requests:

1. To do the Self-Connection Practice one or more times per day for the duration of the immersion year.
2. To have a dyad partner session *at least* once a week for at least two-thirds of the immersion year.
3. To participate in triad practice at least once a week for at least two-thirds of the immersion year.

Daily Self-Connection Practice

MEDITATION (PRACTICING PRESENCE)

Practice for 5 minutes or more each day. Pick a regular time of day and a quiet place. If you already have or have had a meditation practice that you want to use, please do so.

If you do not have one, a very common practice is to place your awareness on your breath, following the in breath and out breath.

When you notice that you have lost awareness of your breathing and that unconscious, automatic, habitual thinking has been happening, gently and compassionately bring your attention back to the breath. Continue doing this for the amount of time you have set aside to meditate.

JACKAL JOURNAL

You can track and translate your judgments of self and others when you notice a strong reaction to something. We suggest getting a dedicated journal or notebook to use just for this purpose.

Here is an example:

Under the heading "Observations," write:
   a) What you observed happening that is the stimulus for how you are feeling.
   b) What thoughts you observe going through your mind as you think about that event *in the present as you are writing.* Be as free-flowing and uncensored as you can with this.
Next, under "Feelings," write:
   a) How you are feeling as you think about the event *in the present as you are writing* (rather than what you were feeling when it happened).
   b) You may want to use the feelings list to strengthen your feeling vocabulary. Be mindful of using faux-feeling language that refers to your thinking rather than to the feelings, sensations, emotions alive inside you.
   c) Also, give yourself some space to really feel how you are feeling. Experience being in your body

awareness, rather than only mentally labeling the feeling.

Next, under "Needs," write:

a) The needs you connect with in relation to your thoughts and feelings. What words or phrases most deeply and satisfyingly resonate?

b) Be mindful of using language that mixes universal needs with specific strategies. We recommend using the needs list that appears earlier in this manual.

c) Again, we request that you take the space to really feel what's happening in your body as you search for the words that best resonate with you, until you feel a shift in your body, a feeling of opening, relaxation, softening, peace, compassion, and connection with yourself and others.

d) Once you have found some language for your needs, try savoring and deepening your connection to them, enjoying and appreciating the ways in which they are significant to you and the richness they bring.

Next, under "Requests," write:

a) Whether you have a specific, doable, action-language request of yourself or of someone else to do something to contribute to your needs (your needs to care for yourself *and* your needs to care for others).

b) Rather than trying to figure it out or working at it in any way, try putting your attention on your needs and see if a request has already emerged or spontaneously arises in your awareness as you are connected with your needs.

c) Write down what emerges. Perhaps a request will not emerge while you are writing, but will pop into your mind later.

NOTES

GRATITUDE PRACTICE

Marshall Rosenberg talks about "gratitude practice" on disc 9 of his *Sounds True* nine-CD set. Here's how I (Ike) typically do it. Upon waking in the morning, I reflect upon the day before and identify something that I or someone else did that day that I am pleased about. I name in my mind, in observation language, what was said or done. With this observation in mind, I check to see how I feel in that moment and what need of mine is being met by remembering this event. I then typically linger for some moments, savoring my gratitude. Sometimes, I'm prompted by my sense of gratitude to communicate my appreciation to the person who was part of the event.

GRATITUDE JOURNAL

The gratitude journal is a written version of the gratitude practice. In the journal you would record what specifically has met your needs—about you, others, life.

WEEKLY DYAD PARTNER SESSIONS

A dyad partner session is a scheduled time with another person for sharing something meaningful in your life and having them support you in identifying the needs met or not met in this particular situation. They provide this support by offering guesses as to your needs. Then you switch roles. These sessions are often done by phone.

Partner dyad practice—skill of empathy
(1 hour each week, or more)

1. Choose who will speak first and who will listen
2. The speaker talks about something she is celebrating or has negative judgments about. The listener does presence, understanding, and need language/deepening (20 minutes).

NOTES

3. Stop and harvest the learning together, give feedback about what you experienced in your role and what helped and what did not (10 minutes).
4. Switch roles and repeat the process.

Another option is that the speaker talks about someone she has an "enemy image" about and goes through the self-empathy Enemy Image Process or the self-expression Enemy Image Process, and the listener supports. We suggest that you use the description of the processes in this manual to support you.

TIMETABLE AND CONTACT DETAILS

Dyad Partner	Contact Details	Date of Session

MEDIATION TRIADS

A triad practice is a scheduled time for practice with two others. Each person gets to sit in the mediator's chair and receive feedback. These 1.5- to 2-hour sessions are often done by phone.

TIMETABLE AND CONTACT DETAILS

Triad Partners	Contact Details	Date of Session

FIRST INTENSIVE PRACTICE REQUESTS

_____

_____

_____

_____

_____

_____

SECOND INTENSIVE PRACTICE REQUESTS

THIRD INTENSIVE PRACTICE REQUESTS

THE INDIVIDUAL ACTION PLAN (IAP)

 The five levels of commitment are think it, share it, do it, teach it, and live it."

—*Jeremy Whitt*

We invite returning participants to create an individual action plan, or IAP. It is a written declaration of your personal learning goals and the specific actions that you will take to reach those goals. We are convinced that the more clearly and thoughtfully you state and track your intentions, the higher the probability that you will achieve them. The list below summarizes one way to create your IAP. We encourage you to use whatever means suits you.

1. Brainstorm about your dreams, expectations, and specific goals connected to the upcoming training.
2. Have an in-depth conversation with another training participant to determine your own training goals and the specific actions you will take to reach them. Try to formulate goals that are measurable and that have a clear time line. Ideally, they will be challenging, yet realistic.
3. Work backward from each goal to devise the concrete steps that will help you achieve it. Record the steps you will take in positive language—emphasizing what you want to do, rather than what you want to avoid doing.

SAMPLE ACTION PLAN
Goal #1: My goal is to start working as a mediator.
Focus area: Networking, finding support from other mediators/training participants.
Step 1. *Mediate real conflict at least once during next training. If real conflict does not arise, then I will request role-play during training session or during break times.*
Step 2. *Request feedback from the trainers and concrete recommendations for improvement.*
Step 3. *Find a place to mediate once training is complete. For this step, I will definitely want the ideas and support of the trainers and other participants.*
Step 4. *Create a support group with other participants and hold regular meetings. I will connect with other current or aspiring mediators to create a group of three to four people. We will have Skype support sessions at least once a week.*

SAMPLE ACTION PLAN

Goal #1: My goal is to be a more efficient parent and a better communicator at home.

Focus area: Receiving mediation support in relation to family issues.

Step 1. *Listen carefully to the training material with an ear for how this can help me with my teenage children. Keep a special journal with my notes, reflections, and discoveries.*

Step 2. *Request a special mediation practice session on parenting themes.*

Step 3. *Get feedback from the trainers and concrete recommendations for improvement.*

Step 4. *Create a support group with at least one other parent. We will have official check-ins by phone every two weeks and, ideally, will also be available for empathy sessions.*

> " Until one is committed there is hesitancy,
> The chance to draw back, always ineffectiveness.
> Concerning all acts of initiative (and creation),
> There is one elementary truth, the ignorance of which
> Kills countless ideas and splendid plans:
> That the moment one definitely commits oneself,
> Then Providence moves too.
> All sorts of things occur to help one
> That would never otherwise have occurred.
> A whole stream of events issues from the decision,
> Raising in one's favor all manner of unforeseen
> Incidents and meetings and material assistance,
> Which no man could have dreamt would have
> Come his way.
> I have learned a deep respect
> For one of Goethe's couplets:
>> Whatever you can do, or dream you can, begin it.
>> Boldness has genius, power, and magic in it."
>
> —*W. H. Murray*, The Scottish Himalayan Expedition

QUESTIONS FOR INDIVIDUAL REFLECTION

The following questions are to help you reflect on your experience of the training and to gain some clarity about what you are committed to taking from this training into your life. They are designed as part of the positive feedback loop described earlier.

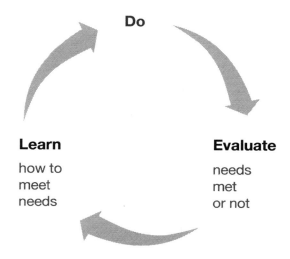

Do

Learn
how to
meet
needs

Evaluate
needs
met
or not

What were the highlights of the training? What did you enjoy? What did you find challenging? Were there any *aha* moments?

What were the most important parts of the training for you and/or the most important things you learned? What needs did the training meet? What do you feel drawn to do more work on?

How does what you have learned relate to where you are right now in life? How does this learning relate to your vision for the future and/or your sense of purpose in life?

What is most important for you to focus on over the next three months, six months, year? What could get in the way, and how can you address that?

What are some of the possible actions you can imagine taking following this retreat? What are you committed to doing?

Chapter 8

Resources

Visit the Mediate Your Life website at **www.mediateyourlife.com**
for a continually updated list of resources.

Learning Nonviolent Communication

Nonviolent Communication: A Language of Life, by Marshall Rosenberg, 2003

Speak Peace in a World of Conflict: What You Say Next Will Change Your World,
by Marshall Rosenberg, 2005

Audio featuring Marshall Rosenberg:

- NVC Training Course (9 CDs)
- Speaking Peace (2 CDs)
- CDs from International Intensive Training with Marshall

Videos featuring Marshall Rosenberg:

- The Basics of Nonviolent Communication (2 DVDs)
- Making Life Wonderful (4 DVDs)

Also search YouTube videos for "Marshall Rosenberg."

The Center for Nonviolent Communication
www.cnvc.org

NVC Academy
http://nvctraining.com

PuddleDancer Press
www.nonviolentcommunication.com

Bay NVC
www.baynvc.org

NVC Boston
http://www.nvcboston.org

Power of Compassion—Houston NVC
http://www.houstonnvc.org/

Growing Compassion
http://www.growingcompassion.org/

Other Resources

Why Nations Fail: The Origins of Power, Prosperity, and Poverty, by Daron Acemoglu and James A. Robinson, 2012

I Thought It Was Just Me (But It Isn't): Making the Journey from "What Will People Think?" to "I Am Enough," by Brené Brown, 2007

See also Brené Brown's TED talk on vulnerability.
http://www.ted.com/talks/brene_brown_on_vulnerability.html

When Things Fall Apart: Heart Advice for Difficult Times, by Pema Chodron, 1997

Comfortable with Uncertainty: 108 Teachings on Cultivating Fearlessness and Compassion, by Pema Chodron, 2010

Taking the Leap: Freeing Ourselves from Old Habits and Fears, by Pema Chodron, 2011

Super Brain: Unleashing the Explosive Power of Your Brain to Maximize Health, Happiness, and Spiritual Well-Being, by Deepak Chopra and Rudolph Tanzi, 2012

The 7 Habits of Highly Effective People: Powerful Lessons in Personal Change, by Stephen R. Covey, 2013

The Power of Habit: Why We Do What We Do in Life and Business, by Charles Duhigg, 2012

Incognito: The Secret Lives of the Brain, by David Eagleman, 2012

Awakening Earth: Exploring the Evolution of Human Culture and Consciousness, by Duane Elgin 1993

The Checklist Manifesto: How to Get Things Right, by Atul Gawande, 2011

Who's in Charge?: Free Will and the Science of the Brain, by Michael Gazzaniga, 2012

Violence: Reflections on a National Epidemic, by James Gilligan, M.D., 1997 (Ike recommends p. 111 on shame as "the most carefully guarded secret held by violent men.")

Moral Tribes: Emotion, Reason, and the Gap Between Them, by Joshua Greene, 2013

On Combat: The Psychology and Physiology of Deadly Conflict in War and in Peace, by Lt. Col. Dave Grossman, 2008 (Ike recommends chapter 2 on the importance of training in the conditions you are expecting to encounter.)

The Righteous Mind: Why Good People Are Divided by Politics and Religion, by Jonathan Haidt, 2013

Hardwiring Happiness: The New Brain Science of Contentment, Calm, and Confidence, by Rick Hanson, 2013

Thinking, Fast and Slow, by Daniel Kahneman, 2011

Loving What Is: Four Questions That Can Change Your Life, by Byron Katie, 2003
See also Byron Katie's website: www.thework.com

What We Say Matters: Practicing Nonviolent Communication, by Judith Hansen Lasater and Ike K. Lasater, 2009.

Words That Work in Business: A Practical Guide to Effective Communication in the Workplace, by Ike Lasater with Julie Stiles, 2010

See also Ike Lasater's Words That Work website (http://wordsthatwork.us/site/resources/articles/) for copious written reflections on NVC by Ike, John Kinyon, and Julie Stiles, including the following:

"Mediation and Mediator Self-Care: A Nonviolent Communication Approach," by Ike Lasater & John Kinyon with Julie Stiles, 2010

"Becoming a Better Mediator by Mediating Your Inner Dialogue," by Ike Lasater and John Kinyon with Julie Stiles, 2009

"The Three-Chair Model for Learning NVC Mediation: Developing Capacity for Mindful Presence, Connection and Skill with NVC," by Ike Lasater and John Kinyon with Julie Stiles, 2009

"Skill Building and Personal Growth Through NVC Mediation Triad Practice," by Ike Lasater with Julie Stiles, 2009

"What is NVC Mediation: A Powerful Model for Healing and Reconciling Conflict," by Ike Lasater with Julie Stiles, 2009

"The Origin and Resolution of Conflict," by Ike Lasater with Julie Stiles, 2008

"Group Decision Making: A Nonviolent Communication Perspective," by Ike Lasater with Julie Stiles, 2008

"The Future of NVC Mediation: Where We Have Been, Where We Are, Where We Might Go," by Ike Lasater with Julie Stiles, 2009

"Using NVC to Make a Living Doing NVC," by Ike Lasater with Julie Stiles, 2009

"NVC Conflict Coaching," by Ike Lasater with Julie Stiles, 2008

"Working with Enemy Images Before and During Mediations," by Ike Lasater with Julie Stiles, 2006

"Accreted Mediation: Building Clarity and Connection," by Ike Lasater with Julie Stiles, 2006

"Working with One Party: A Nonviolent Communication (NVC) Approach to Family Conflicts," by Ike Lasater with Julie Stiles, 2006

The Empathy Factor: Your Competitive Advantage for Personal, Team, and Business Success, by Marie R. Miyashiro, 2011

Self-Compassion: The Proven Power of Being Kind to Yourself, by Kristin Neff, 2011
www.self-compassion.org

See also Kristin Neff's TEDx talk on the space between self-esteem and self-compassion.
http://www.youtube.com/watch?v=IvtZBUSplr4

Words Can Change Your Brain: 12 Conversation Strategies to Build Trust, Resolve Conflict, and Increase Intimacy, by Andrew Newberg and Mark Robert Waldman, 2012

Change Anything: The New Science of Personal Success, by Kerry Patterson, Joseph Grenny, David Maxfield, Ron McMillan, Al Switzler, 2012

A Way of Being, by Carl Rogers, 1980

On Becoming a Person, by Carl Rogers, 1961

On Personal Power: Inner Strength and its Revolutionary Impact, by Carl Rogers, 1977

The Four Agreements: A Practical Guide to Personal Freedom, by Don Miguel Ruiz, 1997

The I of the Storm: Embracing Conflict, Creating Peace, by Gary Simmons, 2001

Parenting without Power Struggles, by Susan Stiffelman, 2010

A New Earth: Awakening to Your Life's Purpose, by Eckhart Tolle, 2005

The Power of Now: A Guide to Spiritual Empowerment, by Eckhart Tolle, 2004

Stillness Speaks, by Eckhart Tolle, 2003

For video, visit www.eckharttolletv.com.
Also search www.oprah.com for "Eckhart Tolle."

Pilgrim (2012) and other books of poetry by David Whyte
http://www.davidwhyte.com/

The Third Side: Why We Fight and How We Can Stop by William L. Ury (Sep 1, 2000)

Getting To Yes: Negotiating an Agreement Without Giving In, by Roger Fisher, William L. Ury and Bruce Patton, 2011

A Theory of Everything: An Integral Vision for Business, Politics, Science and Spirituality, by Ken Wilbur, 2000

Integral Life Practice: A 21st-Century Blueprint for Physical Health, Emotional Balance, Mental Clarity, and Spiritual Awakening, by Ken Wilbur, 2008

See also Ken Wilbur's website: www.integrallife.com

Mindfulness: An Eight-Week Plan for Finding Peace in a Frantic World, by Mark Williams, Danny Penman, Jon Kabat-Zinn, 2012

Chapter 9

Appendix

A. KEY ASPECTS OF OUR TRAINING

PERSONAL GROWTH

To upgrade your internal operating system and grow your capacity, we recommend that you put your own conflicts and situations "into the chairs." We believe that by doing this you will develop not only skills but also capacity to respond as you would like to conflict and intensity.

IMPORTANCE OF PRACTICE

We see the workshops as a place to be inspired, create community, and learn options for what and how to practice, but we see the real learning, growth, and change happening through what you do (i.e., practice) on a daily and weekly basis.

GIVING AND RECEIVING FEEDBACK

Feedback is an essential component of learning and change. In the training we see it as a kind of "biofeedback"—we describe our internal biological experience in relation to another's actions. We see two key aspects to this: 1) tell the person *specifically* what did or didn't meet your needs (i.e., the observations) and 2) *speak from your internal experience and feelings,* rather than from your thoughts/evaluations. Also, we've found it very helpful to *start with what you did like, then give the person a choice* about your expressing what you didn't like and what would have worked better for you.

SELF-APPROPRIATED LEARNING

We have been deeply inspired by American psychologist Carl Rogers regarding learning. In this training we offer you certain skills and processes that we've found valuable. We would like you to try what we offer to see if it works for you. If it doesn't, experiment and change it until it does. Then tell us about it so we can learn from your experience.

INTENSIVE-SPEAK

The way we trainers speak and demonstrate in the intensives is based on how to best support participants to learn and practice the skills. It comes out of decades of NVC workshop experience. Participants sometimes ask for ways of expressing that others in their lives can relate to more easily. There are probably infinite subculture contexts in which you may want to use or offer these skills. We encourage you to discover language that will connect you with the people you want to reach.

B. IMMERSION PROGRAM: MAPS OVERVIEW

1. Internal
   a) Self-connection practice and intensity practice **(SCP/IP)**
   b) Internal mediation **(IM)**
   c) Chooser-educator **(C-E)**

2. Interpersonal
   d) Enemy Image Process—self-empathy **(EIP-SE)**
   e) Interpersonal mediation model **(IPM)**
   f) Healing and reconciliation—making amends **(H&R/MA)**
   g) Mourn/celebrate/learn—self-empathy **(MCL-SE)**
   h) Celebrate/mourn/learn **(CML)**

3. Formal/informal between others (including with groups)
   i) EIP—empathy/pre-mediation **(EIP-Emp)**
   j) EIP—role-play **(EIP-RP)**
   k) Mediation model **(MM)**—Formal and informal versions
   l) Healing and reconciliation, healing role-play **(H&R/RP)**
   m) Mourn/celebrate/learn—empathy/post-mediation **(MCL-Emp)**
   n) Engagement conversation (three parts)
   o) Group mediation model
   p) Group decision-making process

C. TRIAD "DRY PRACTICE" SKILLS 3–5 AND 9

SKILL-DRILL EXERCISES
Skill 3, pulling by the ears, version 1: Example
   1. Mediator: "Person A, do you have a need you'd like B to hear?"

2. Person A: "Respect."

3. Mediator: "Person B, are you willing to tell A what you heard?"

4. Person B: "I heard that A thinks I'm disrespectful."

5. Mediator: "Thank you for saying what you heard. I heard A wants respect. Are you willing to tell A what you heard she wants?"

6. Person B: "A wants respect."

7. Mediator: "Thank you."

Skill 3, pulling by the ears, version 2: Example

1. Mediator: "Person A, do you have a need you'd like B to hear?"

2. Person A: "Trust."

3. Mediator: "Person B, are you willing to tell A what you heard?"

4. Person B: "I think trust is a two-way street."

5. Mediator: "I want to hear what you think, B. First, though, are you willing to tell A what you heard she wants? I heard she wants trust."

6. Person B: "A wants trust."

7. Mediator: "Thank you."

Skills 4 and 5, emergency first-aid empathy and tracking: Example

1. Mediator: "Person A, do you have a need you'd like B to hear?"

2. Person A: "Love."

3. Mediator: "Person B, are you willing to tell A what you heard?"

4. Person B: "How can I love someone who is so inconsiderate!"

5. Mediator: "So, B, sounds like you have a strong need for consideration that isn't being met. Is that right?"

6. Person B: "Yes."

7. Mediator: "I want to hear more about that, B. First, though, are you willing to tell A what you heard she wants? I heard she wants love."

8. Person B: "Okay, A wants love."

Skill 9, solution requests, need behind the no (NBN)

1. Find a real situation to work with and a person A.

2. Mediator asks A what her needs are in this situation. Clarify together.

3. Mediator asks A what she thinks person B's needs are. Clarify with B.

4. Mediator asks A what request she has of B. Supports A in making request.

5. B in some way says no. Mediator empathizes with needs behind the no.

6. Mediator asks B for request to meet his needs. Supports B to make request.

7. Either A says yes or continue with NBN process.

D. ENEMY IMAGE PROCESS (EIP) WORKSHEET

The Three Parts of the Enemy Image Process
(preparation for conversation/taking action)

We define an "enemy image" as any barrier to feeling connection and compassion with someone. A key component to this process is cycling within part 1 (between observations, feelings, needs) and between parts 1, 2, and 3.

1. Self-empathy—unmet needs of self in relation to other's actions
2. Empathy for other—connect to other's needs that may be behind their actions
3. Emergence of new possibilities to meet needs (learning, planning, practice)

1. Self-empathy

a) **Observation:** Thinking of the person with whom you have an enemy image and want to be able to take effective action, write your observation of what happened and your thoughts, judgments, and evaluations about the person, including the story you are telling yourself, and possibly your core beliefs about yourself, others, life.

What you heard/saw them say/do was . . .

Your thoughts, judgments, evaluations, and story/core beliefs are . . .

b) **Feelings and needs:** Translate your thoughts/judgments, connect to feelings and needs.

First, feel your emotional reactions. How are you feeling right now as you think about the person or event? Be aware of faux feelings and translate them into internal, bodily emotions and sensations. Give yourself space to connect to and feel your body awareness, rather than only conceptually labeling the feeling. (Use the feelings list if it helps.)

Your feelings:

Next, connect your thoughts and feelings to needs until you feel a shift in your body, a quality of relaxation, peace, and compassion. List the needs that resonate for you. (Use the needs list if it helps.)

Your needs:

c) **Cycling:** As you move to connecting with feelings and needs, you may notice more judgments and reactions. If so, cycle, or loop, from observing your thoughts to connecting with feelings and needs.

2. Empathy for other (understanding and needs)
As you move toward empathizing with the other's needs, you may get triggered into more judgments and emotional reactions. If this happens, cycle back to part 1 until you feel reconnected to your needs, then try coming back to part 2. Cycle back and forth as needed. This cycling also applies to moving between parts 1, 2, and 3.

a) **Guessing understanding and needs of the other:** Imagine the thoughts, feelings, and needs they might be having that might be motivating the behavior that is not meeting your needs. Do this for yourself, to contribute to your own peace, well-being, and effectiveness in responding, rather than thinking you need to know what's actually true for them. Focus on what gives you an increased feeling of relaxation, space, and openness, as well as understanding, compassion, and connection to the person. This does not mean you agree with or condone their behavior.

Person's possible thoughts, feelings and needs:

b) Holding together in your mind the needs of self and other: This step is about bringing together in your consciousness your needs and their needs, saying to yourself all the needs and seeing that you and another have in common human needs that we all share.

Your needs and their needs:

3. Emergence of new possibilities, solutions, requests (learn, plan, practice)

a) Learning: From this internal connection with self and other, do any new ideas, insights, or possibilities arise in you? See if you can form a specific, doable, action-language (what you do want) request or requests of yourself, the other person, or anyone else. Also, in forming this request/strategy, are you seeking to meet your needs and the other person's?

b) Planning/practice: After forming a request, you can plan what you want to say or do in relation to the person. If this involves a conversation with them, you can practice what you might actually say and also how you might deal with their response. One way to do this is to role-play a practice conversation, for example with a coach or a dyad partner, or by journaling.

What is your plan of what to do now, "on the other side of connection"? Do you have requests of yourself, the other person, or someone else? You could have a request of yourself to choose a new belief/story through use of a Byron Katie "turnaround."

E. MOURN/CELEBRATE/LEARN (MCL) WORKSHEET

The Three Parts of the Mourn/Celebrate/Learn (MCL) Process

The MCL process is about learning from conversations and/or taking action. A key component of this learning process is a cycling between its three parts. The typical "learning cycle" seeks to avoid blame and punishment: we move from "doing" to a moralistic evaluation of that doing (is it right or wrong, good or bad?), and then to learning and planning how to avoid blame and punishment in the future and how to seek what will be rewarded by others. But we can instead choose a learning cycle that seeks to move toward what better meets our needs: we move from "doing" to a needs-based evaluation (mourning needs not met and celebrating needs met), and then to learning and planning how to better meet our needs in the future.

1. Mourn needs not met by what we did and what happened.

Observe what happened

   a) What you did and what happened that you're evaluating

   b) Your thoughts, judgments, evaluations, and story/core beliefs

Feelings and needs of mourning (from anger/guilt/shame to "natural" sadness)

   a) Feel your emotional reactions. How are you feeling right now as you think about what happened? Be aware of faux feelings and translate them into internal, bodily emotions and sensations (use the feelings handout if this helps).

   Your feelings:

b) Connect your thoughts and feelings to needs until you feel a shift in your body from anger, guilt, shame, etc. to sadness (use the needs list if this helps).

Your needs:

Cycling: As you move to connecting with feelings and needs, you may notice more judgments and reactions. If so, cycle from observing your thoughts to connecting with feelings and needs. As you move toward empathizing with needs that were met or attempted to be met, you may get triggered into more judgments and emotional reactions. If this happens, cycle back to steps 1–3, then try coming back to step 4. This cycling also applies to steps 5 and 6.

2. Celebrate or appreciate needs met or that we tried to meet with what happened. Try to find any possible needs that were met by what happened. Explore possibilities until you feel a sense of peace, well-being, relaxation, and compassion/understanding. This does not mean you agree with or like what you or another did or what happened.

Needs met:

Hold together in your mind the needs met and not met. This step is about bringing together in your consciousness all your needs related to this situation.

Needs met and not met:

3. Learn from what happened, devising new strategies for better meeting needs.

a) Learning: From this internal connection with needs met and not met, do any new ideas, insights, or possibilities arise in you? Thinking back on what happened, what would you do now that might better meet *all* of your needs?

b) Planning: Can you think of any ways to support or reinforce new strategies for meeting your needs in the future?

Ideas/plans:

F. MY CONFLICTS

DESCRIPTION	Conflict	Parties Involved	Duration	Intensity
	Give your conflict enough of a description that you can recognize and remember it later.	*Again, to help you remember the conflict later.*	*How long has this conflict been going on? Is it new or has it been going on for months or even years? Is it long-standing, ongoing, frequent, fleeting?*	*5 = Painful* *4 = Draining* *3 = Distracting* *2 = Irritating* *1 = Bothersome*
SAMPLE	A colleague often interrupts me in meetings. I don't think he cares about my ideas.	Me and A.Z.	Pops up every few weeks for the last 1.5 years	3
1)				
2)				
3)				
4)				
5)				

G. MY CONFLICT HABITS

DESCRIPTION	Habits *A brief description of your habit.*	Cue *In what situation does this happen?*	Routine *What actions do you take?*	Reward *What is the reward you seek with this habit?*	New Routine *What new routine could I use to replace the old one?*
SAMPLE	I smile when I am in conflict.	I am in a conflict and am embarrassed about being in the conflict.	I listen to another person and smile.	I feel safe—like this is "no big deal."	Be more authentic: Say, "I'm not comfortable with this conversation and would like to come back to it in 10 minutes."
1)					
2)					
3)					
4)					
5)					

Made in the USA
San Bernardino,
CA